Menaechmi;
Or, The Twin-Brothers

By Plautus

Translated by Henry Thomas Riley

A Digireads.com Book
Digireads.com Publishing
16212 Riggs Rd
Stilwell, KS, 66085

Menaechmi; Or, The Twin-Brothers
By Plautus
Translated by Henry Thomas Riley
ISBN: 1-4209-2906-2

Please visit *www.digireads.com*

DRAMATIS PERSONAE.

MENAECHMUS of Epidamnus.
MENAECHMUS SOSICLES, his twin-brother.
PENICULUS, a Parasite.
MESSENIO, the servant of Menaechmus Sosicles.
CYLINDRUS, a Cook.
AN OLD MAN, father-in-law of Menaechmus Sosicles.
A DOCTOR.

THE WIFE OF MENAECHMUS of Epidamnus.
EROTIUM, a Courtesan.
MAID-SERVANT of Erotium.

> (*Scene—Epidamnus, a city of Illyricum. The house of*
> MENAECHMUS *of Epidamnus is on one side of the street,*
> *and that of* EROTIUM *on the other.*)

4

INTRODUCTION.

THE SUBJECT.

MOSCHUS, a merchant of Syracuse, had two twin sons who exactly resembled each other. One of these, whose name was Menaechmus, when a child, accompanied his father to Tarentum, at which place he was stolen and carried away to Epidamnus, where in course of time he has married a wealthy wife. Disagreements, however, arising with her, he forms an acquaintance with the Courtesan Erotium, and is in the habit of presenting her with clothes and jewels which he pilfers from his wife. The original name of the other twin-brother was Sosicles, but on the loss of Menaechmus, the latter name has been substituted by their grandfather for Sosicles, in remembrance of the lost child. Menaechmus Sosicles, on growing to manhood, determines to seek his lost brother. Having wandered for six years, lie arrives at Epidamnus, attended by his servant, Messenio. In consequence of his resemblance to his brother, many curious and laughable mistakes happen between him and the Courtesan Erotium, the wife of Menaechmus of Epidamnus, the Cook Cylindrus, the Parasite Peniculus, the father-in-law of Menaechmus of Epidamnus, and lastly Messenio himself. At length, through the agency of the latter, the brothers recognize each other; on which Messenio receives his liberty, and Menaechmus of Epidamnus resolves to make sale of his possessions and to return to Syracuse, his native place.

THE ACROSTIC ARGUMENT.

[Supposed to have been written by Priscian the Grammarian.]

A SICILIAN merchant (Mercator) who had two sons, on one being stolen from him (Ei), ended his life. As a name (Nomen) for him who is at home, his paternal grandfather (Avus) gives him that of Menaechmus instead of Sosicles. And (Et) he, as soon as he is grown up, goes to seek his brother about (Circum) all countries. At last he comes to Epidamnus; hither (Huc) the one that was stoien has been carried. All think that the stranger, Menaechmus (Menaechmum), is their fellow-citizen, and address him (Eum) as such: Courtesan, wife, and father-in-law. There (Ibi) at last the brothers mutually recognize each other.

THE PROLOGUE.

In the first [1] place now, Spectators, at the commencement, do I wish health and happiness [2] to myself and to you. I bring you Plautus, with my tongue, not with my hand: I beg that you will receive him with favouring ears. Now learn the argument, and give your attention; in as few words as possible will I be brief. And, in fact, this subject is a Greek one; still, it is not an Attic [3], but a Sicilian one. But in their Comedies the poets do this; they feign that all the business takes place at Athens [4], in order that it may appear the more Grecian to you. I will not tell you that this matter happened anywhere except where it is said to have happened. This has been my preface to the subject of this play. Now will I give the subject, meted out to you, not in a measure, nor yet in a threefold measure [5], but in the granary itself; so great is my heartiness in telling you the plot.

There was a certain aged man, a merchant at Syracuse [6]; to him two sons were born, twins, children so like in appearance that their own foster-mother [7], who gave the breast, was not able to distinguish them, nor even the mother herself who had given them birth; as a person, indeed, informed me who had seen the children; I never saw them, let no one of you fancy so. After the children were now seven years old, the father freighted a large ship with much merchandize. The father put one of the twins on board the ship, and took him away, together with himself, to traffic at Tarentum [8]; the other one he left with his mother at home. By accident, there were games at Tarentum when he came there: many persons, as generally happens at the games, had met together; the child strayed away there from his father among the people. A certain merchant of Epidamnus was there; he picked up the child, and carried it away to Epidamnus [9]. But its father, after he had lost the child, took it heavily to heart, and through grief at it he died a few days after at Tarentum. Now, after news reached the grandfather of the children at home about this matter, how that one of the children had been stolen, the grandfather changed the name of that other twin. So much did he love that one which had been stolen, that he gave his name to the one that was at home. That you may not mistake hereafter, I tell you then this beforehand; the name of both the twin-brothers is the same. He gave the same name of Menaechmus to this one as the other had; and by the same name the grandfather himself was called. I remember his name the more easily for the reason that I saw him cried with much noise [10]. Now must I speed back on foot to Epidamnus, that I may exactly disclose this matter to you. If any one of you [11] wishes anything to be transacted for him at Epidamnus, command me boldly and speak out; but on these terms, that he give me the means by which it may be transacted for him. For unless a person gives the money, he will be mistaken; (*in a lower tone*) except that he who does give it will be very much more mistaken [12]. But I have returned to that place whence I set forth, and yet I am standing in the self-same spot. This person of Epidamnus, whom I mentioned just now, that stole that other twin child, had no children, except his wealth. He adopted as his son the child so carried off, and gave him a well-portioned wife, and made him his heir when he himself died. For as, by chance, he was going into the country, when it had rained heavily, entering, not far from the city, a rapid stream, in its rapidity [13] it threw the ravisher of the child off his legs; and hurried the man away to great and grievous destruction. And so a very large fortune fell to that youth. Here (*pointing to the house*) does the stolen twin *now* dwell. Now that twin, who dwells at Syracuse, has come this day to Epidamnus with his servant to make enquiry for this own twin-brother of his. This is the city of Epidamnus while this play is acting; when another shall be acted, it will become another town; just as our companies, too, are wont to be shifted about. The same person now acts the procurer, now the youth, now the old man, the pauper, the beggar, the king, the parasite, the soothsayer * * * * *

FOOTNOTES TO THE PROLOGUE.

[1] In the first: This Play was the foundation of Shakespeare's Comedy of Errors. See the Note at the end of the Play.

[2] Health and happiness: "Salutem propitiam." Literally, "propitious health."

[3] It is not an Attic: "Graecissat, Atticissat, Sicelissat." Perhaps these words might be more literally translated, "Graecize," "Atticize," and "Sicilicize."

[4] At Athens: As the majority of the Greek Comic Poets were either natives of, or residents at, Athens, they would naturally take that extensive, opulent, and bustling city as the scene of many of their Comedies. In the time of Plautus, Greek was yet the language of the Sicilians. In Cicero's time the language of the Sicilians was a mixture, partly Greek and partly Latin. Apuleius informs us that in his day they spoke Greek, Latin, and a language peculiar to themselves, called the Sicilian.

[5] A threefold measure: "Trimodius." This was a measure for corn, consisting of three "modii," which last contained about a peck of English measure.

[6] At Syracuse: Syracuse was the principal city of Sicily famed for its commerce and opulence.

[7] Foster-mother: "Mater." Literally, "mother."

[8] At Tarentum: Tarentum was a city of Calabria, in the south of Italy. It was said to have been founded by the Lacedaemonians.

[9] To Epidamnus: Epidamnus, or Epidamnum, was a town of Macedonia, situate on the Adriatic Sea. It was much resorted to for the purpose of transit to the opposite shores of Italy. It received its original name from Epidamnus, one of its kings but on falling into the possession of the Romans, they changed its name, as we are informed by Pliny the Elder, into Dyrrachium, from a superstitious notion that when hey were going to "Epidamnum," they were going "to their loss," as "damnum" is the Latin for "loss" or "destruction," and "epi" is the Greek preposition signifying "to." Cicero was banished to this place.

[10] Cried with much noise: Probably the word "flagitarier" means that the lost child was cried publicly by the "praeco," or "crier."

[11] If any one of you: This is said facetiously to the Audience for the purpose of catching a laugh.

[12] Very much more mistaken: Because he will keep the money and not execute the commission.

[13] In its rapidity: He means to pun upon the words "rapidus," rapid" or "carrying away," and "raptor," the "carrier away" or "ravisher." "The stream carried away the carrier away"

10

ACT I.

SCENE I.

Enter PENICULUS.

PENICULUS. The young men have given me the name of Peniculus [1], for this reason, because when I eat, I wipe the tables clean. * * * * * The persons who bind captives with chains, and who put fetters upon runaway slaves, act very foolishly, in my opinion at least. For if bad usage is added to his misfortune for a wretched man, the greater is his inclination to run away and to do amiss. For by some means or other do they release themselves from the chains; while thus fettered, they either wear away a link with a file, or else with a stone they knock out the nail; 'tis a mere trifle this. He whom you wish to keep securely that he may not run away, with meat and with drink ought he to be chained; do you bind down the mouth of a man to a full table. So long as you give him what to eat and what to drink at his own pleasure in abundance every day, i' faith he'll never run away, even if he has committed an offence that's capital; easily will you secure him so long as you shall bind him with such chains. So very supple are these chains of food, the more you stretch them so much the more tightly do they bind. But now I'm going directly to Menaechmus; whither for this long time I have been sentenced, thither of my own accord I am going, that he may enchain me. For, by my troth, this man does not nourish persons, but he quite rears and reinvigorates them; no one administers medicine more agreeably. Such is this young man; himself with a very well-stocked larder, he gives dinners fit for Ceres [2]; so does he heap the tables up, and piles so vast of dishes does he arrange, you must stand on your couch if you wish for anything at the top. But I have now had an interval these many days, while I've been lording it at home all along together with my dear ones [3];—for nothing do I eat or purchase but what it is most dear. But inasmuch as dear ones, when they are provided, are in the habit of forsaking us, I am now paying him a visit. But his door is opening; and see, 1 perceive Menaechmus himself; he is coming out of doors.

SCENE II.

Enter MENAECHMUS *of Epidamnus, from his house.*

MENAECHMUS of Epidamnus. (*speaking at the door to his* WIFE *within*) . Unless you were worthless, unless you were foolish, unless you were stark wild and an idiot, that which you see is disagreeable to your husband, you would deem to be so to yourself as well. Moreover, if after this day you do any such thing to me, I'll force you, a divorced woman, turned out of my doors to go visit your father. For as often as I wish to go out of the house, you are detaining me, calling me back, asking me questions; whither I am going, what matter I am about, what business I am transacting, what I am wanting, what I am bringing, what I have been doing out of doors? I've surely brought home a custom-house officer [4] as my wife; so much am I obliged to disclose all my business, whatever I have done and am doing. I've had you hitherto indulged too much. Now, therefore, I'll tell you how I am about to act. Since I find you handsomely in maids, provisions, wool, gold trinkets, garments, and purple, and you are wanting in nought, you'll beware of a mischief if you're wise; you'll leave off watching your husband. (*In a lower voice.*) And therefore, that you mayn't be watching me in vain, for your pains I shall find me a mistress to-day, and invite her to dinner somewhere out of doors.

PENICULUS (*apart*). This fellow pretends that he's upbraiding his wife, but he's addressing myself; for if he does dine out of doors, he really is punishing me, not his wife.

MENAECHMUS of Epidamnus. (*to himself*) . Hurra! I' troth, by my taunts I've driven my wife from the door at last. Where now are your intriguing husbands? Why do they hesitate, all returning thanks, to bring presents to me who have fought so gallantly? This mantle [5] of my wife's (*taking it from under his cloak*) I've just now stolen from in-doors, and I'm taking it to my mistress. This way it's proper for a clever trick to be played this knowing husband-watcher. This is a becoming action, this is right, this is skilful, this is done in workman-like style; inasmuch as at my own risk I've taken this from my plague, this same shall be carried off to destruction [6]. With the safety of my allies [7] I've gained a booty from the foe.

PENICULUS (*aloud, at a distance*). Harkye! young man; pray what share have I [8] in that booty?

MENAECHMUS of Epidamnus. I'm undone; I've fallen into an ambuscade.

PENICULUS. Say a safeguard rather. Don't be afraid.

MENAECHMUS of Epidamnus. What person's this?

PENICULUS. 'Tis I. (*Coming up to him.*)

MENAECHMUS of Epidamnus. O my convenient friend—O my ready occasion, save you.

PENICULUS. And save you. (*they shake hands.*)

MENAECHMUS of Epidamnus. What are you about?

PENICULUS. Holding my good Genius in my right hand.

MENAECHMUS of Epidamnus. You couldn't have come to me more à propos than you have come.

MENAECHMUS of Epidamnus. I'm in the habit of doing so; I understand all the points of ready occasion.

MENAECHMUS of Epidamnus. Would you like to be witness of a brilliant exploit?

PENICULUS. What cook has cooked it? I shall know at once if he has made any mistake, when I see the remnants. [9]

MENAECHMUS of Epidamnus. Tell me—did you ever see a picture painted on a wall, where the eagle is carrying off Ganymede [10], or Venus Adonis?

PENICULUS. Many a time. But what are these pictures to me?

MENAECHMUS of Epidamnus. Come, look at me [11]. Do I at all bear any resemblance to them?

PENICULUS. What's this garb of yours?

MENAECHMUS of Epidamnus. Pronounce me to be a very clever fellow.

PENICULUS. Where are we to feed?

MENAECHMUS of Epidamnus. Only do you say that which I requested you.

PENICULUS. Well, I do say so; very clever fellow.

MENAECHMUS of Epidamnus. And don't you venture to add anything of your own to it?

PENICULUS—And very pleasant fellow.

MENAECHMUS of Epidamnus. Go on.

PENICULUS. I' faith, I really can't go on, unless I know for what reason. You've had a fall-out with your wife; on that ground am I the more strongly on my guards [12] against you.

MENAECHMUS of Epidamnus. While you are interrupting me, you are delaying yourself.

PENICULUS. Knock out my only eye [13], Menaechmus, if I speak one word but what you bid me.

MENAECHMUS of Epidamnus. * * * * * where, unknown to my wife, we will erect the funeral pile * * * * * and let us consume this day [14] upon it.

PENICULUS. Well, come then, since you request what's fair, how soon am I to set fire to the pile? Why really, the day's half dead already down to its navel [15].

MENAECHMUS of Epidamnus. Come this way from the door.

PENICULUS. Be it so. (*Moves from the door.*)

MENAECHMUS of Epidamnus. Come still more this way.

PENICULUS Very well. (*Moves.*)

MENAECHMUS of Epidamnus. Even still, step aside boldly from the lioness's den.

PENICULUS (*still moving*). Well done; by my troth, as I fancy, you really would bean excellent charioteers [16].

MENAECHMUS of Epidamnus. Why so?

PENICULUS. That your wife mayn't follow you, you are looking back ever and anon.

MENAECHMUS of Epidamnus. But what say you?

PENICULUS. What, I? Why, whatever you choose, that same do I say, and that same do I deny.

MENAECHMUS of Epidamnus. Could you make any conjecture at all from the smell, if perchance you were to take a smell at something?

PENICULUS. Were the college of Augurs summoned * * * * *

MENAECHMUS of Epidamnus. (*holds out the skirt of the mantle*) . Come then, take a sniff at this mantle that I'm holding. What does it smell of? Do you decline?

PENICULUS. It's as well to smell the top of a woman's garment; for at this other place the nose is offended with an odour that can't be washed out.

MENAECHMUS of Epidamnus. (*holding another part*) . Take a smell here then, Peniculus, as you are so daintily nice.

PENICULUS. Very well. (*He smells it.*)

MENAECHMUS How now? What does it smell of? Answer me.

PENICULUS. Theft, a mistress, and a breakfast. To you * * * * *

MENAECHMUS of Epidamnus. You have spoken out * * * * * now it shall be taken to this mistress of mine, the Courtesan Erotium. I'll order a breakfast at once to be got ready, for me, you, and her; then will we booze away even to the morrow's morning star.

PENICULUS. Capital. You've spoken out distinctly. Am I to knock at the door then?

MENAECHMUS of Epidamnus. Knock—or hold, rather.

PENICULUS. You've removed [17] the goblet a full mile by that.

MENAECHMUS of Epidamnus. Knock gently.

PENICULUS. You're afraid, I think, that the doors are made of Samian crockery. (*Goes to knock.*)

MENAECHMUS of Epidamnus. Hold, prithee, hold, i' faith; see, she's coming out herself. (*The door of* EROTIUM'S *house is opened.*) Ha you behold the sun, is it not quite darkened in comparison with the bright rays of her person.

SCENE III.

Enter EROTIUM, *from her house.*

EROTIUM. My life, Menaechmus, save you.

PENICULUS. And what for me?

EROTIUM. You are out of my number.

PENICULUS. * * * * * that same thing is wont to be done for the other supernumeraries [18] of the legion.

MENAECHMUS of Epidamnus. I would order a skirmish to be got ready there at your house for me to-day.

EROTIUM. To-day it shall be done.

MENAECHMUS of Epidamnus. In that skirmish we two shall drink. Him shall you choose that shall be found there the better warrior with the goblet; do you make up your mind with which of the two you'll pass this night. How much, my love, when I look upon you, do I hate my wife.

EROTIUM. Meantime, however, you cannot help being wrapped in something of hers. What's this? (*Takes hold of the mantle.*)

MENAECHMUS of Epidamnus. (*taking it off*) . 'Tis a new dress for you, and a spoil from [19] my wife, my rosebud.

EROTIUM. You have a ready way of prevailing, so as to be superior in my eyes to any one of those that pay me suit. (*Embraces him.*)

PENICULUS. (*aside*). The harlot's coaxing in the meantime, while she's looking out what to plunder * * * * * (*to* EROTLUM) for if you really loved him, by this his nose ought to have been off with your teething him. [20].

MENAECHMUS of Epidamnus. Take hold of this, Peniculus: I wish to dedicate the spoil that I've vowed.

PENICULUS. Give it me. (*Holds it while* MENAECHMUS *puts it on.*) But, i' faith, prithee, do dance afterwards with the mantle on in this way.

MENAECHMUS of Epidamnus. I—dance? I' faith, you're not in your senses.

PENICULUS. Are you or I the most? If you won't dance, then take it off.

MENAECHMUS of Epidamnus. (*to* EROTIUM) . At a great risk have I stolen this to-day. In my opinion, indeed, Hercules didn't ever carry off the belt from Hippolyta [21] with danger as great. Take this for yourself (he takes it off, and gives her the mantle), since you are the only one alive that's compliant with my humours.

EROTIUM. With such feelings 'tis proper that real lovers should be animated.

PENICULUS. (*aside*) . Those, indeed, who are making haste to bring themselves down to beggary.

MENAECHMUS of Epidamnus. I purchased that for my wife a year since at the price of four minae.

PENICULUS. (*aside*) . The four minae are clearly gone for ever, as the account now stands.

MENAECHMUS of Epidamnus. Do you know what I wish you to attend to?

EROTIUM. I don't know; but I'll attend to whatever you do wish.

MENAECHMUS of Epidamnus. Order a breakfast, then, to be provided for us three at your house, and some dainties to be purchased at the market; kernels of boars' neck, or bacon off the gammon [22], or pig's head, or something in that way, which, when cooked and placed on table before me, may promote an appetite like a kite's: and—forthwith——

EROTIUM. I' faith, I will.

MENAECHMUS of Epidamnus. We're going to the Forum: we shall be here just now. While it's cooking, we'll take a whet in the meantime.

EROTIUM. Come when you like, the things shall be ready.

MENAECHMUS of Epidamnus. Only make haste, then. Do you follow me (*to* PENICULUS).

PENICULUS. By my troth, I certainly shall keep an eye on you, and follow you. I wouldn't take the wealth of the Gods to lose you this day. (*Exeunt* MENAECHMUS *and* PENICULUS.)

EROTIUM. (*speaking at the door of her house*). Call Cylindrus, the cook, out of doors this moment from within.

SCENE IV.

Enter CYLINDRUS, *from the house.*

EROTIUM. Take a hand-basket and some money. See, you have three didrachmns here. (*Giving him money.*)

CYLINDRUS. I have so.

EROTIUM. Go and bring some provisions, see that there's enough for three; let it be neither deficient nor overmuch.

CYLINDRUS. What sort of persons are these to be?

EROTIUM. Myself, Menaechmus, and his Parasite.

CYLINDRUS. Then these make ten, for the Parasite easily performs the duty of eight persons [23].

EROTIUM. I've now told you the guests; do you take care of the rest.

CYLINDRUS. Very well. It's cooked already; bid them go and take their places.

EROTIUM. Make haste back.

CYLINDRUS. I'll be here directly. (*Exit* CYLINDRUS, *and* EROTIUM *goes into her house.*)

FOOTNOTES TO ACT I.

[1] Name of Peniculus: This word means "a sponge" which was fastened to a stick, and was used for the purpose of cleansing tables. He says that the youths so called him from his own propensity for clearing the tables of their provisions. The tails of foxes and of oxen were also used as "peniculi." Colman and Warner, in their translations of Terence and Plautus, render the word "dishclout."

[2] Fit for Ceres: As Ceres was the Goddess of corn and the giver of plenty, the entertainments in honor of her would of course be very bounteous.

[3] With my dear ones: "Cum caris meis." When he says this, it might be supposed that he is meaning his family by these words of endearment. The next line shows that such is not the case. He has had a supply of victuals, purchased at his own cost; he has been consuming these victuals, and right dear (carissimum) has he found them. He is now coming out to look for Menaechmus, and to make up for lost time.

[4] A custom-house officer: The "portitores" examined those who landed or embarked at any port, to see that they had no merchandize about them which had not paid duty. They also made the necessary enquiries who the parties were, and what was their destination. He compares his wife to one of these inquisitive persons

[5] This mantle: The "palla," a kind of "mantle" or "cloak," was worn indifferently by both sexes among the Greeks and Romans. This will account for the circumstance of Menaechmus Sosicles wearing, as we shall see in the sequel, the "palla" of a female, without expecting to attract the notice of passers-by. The "palla," which by the prose writers is also called "pallium," was used for many other purposes than that of a garment. See Dr. Smith's Dictionary of Greek and Roman Antiquities.

[6] To destruction: "Ad damnum." He calls the Courtesan "damnum," sheer loss" or "wastefulness" *par éminence*.

[7] Of my allies: By these he means the Courtesan Erotium and the Parasite Peniculus, who have run no risk by helping him to filch away the mantle.

[8] What share have I: Thinking himself alluded to as one of the "socii" or "allies," the Parasite immediately appears before him and asks what share, then, he is to have of the booty.

[9] When I see the remnants: He thinks that Menaechmus is alluding to something in the eating way, and says that he can tell whether the cook has done his duty well or not, by only looking at the scraps of the entertainment.

[10] Ganymede: He is mentioned in the text under another name of a gross nature. Ganymede was the son of Tros, King of Troy. Jupiter was said, in the form of an eagle, to have carried him off, and made him cupbearer to the Gods, in the place of Hebe, the Goddess of youth.

[11] Come, look at me: Saying this, he probably takes the "palla" from behind him, and putting it on, stalks about with it upon him. This he could do without the risk of being seen by his wife, as on the Roman stage a number of streets and lanes were seen to terminate, up which the actor would go a little way to escape observation from a house situate just at the end of another street. He means to ask the Parasite if he does not quite equal Ganymede or Adonis, as represented in the pictures, by reason of his tasteful attire.

[12] On my guard: As Menaechmus has fallen out with his wife, the Parasite thinks there is no chance of a "coena" at his house. He is the more careful then to make enquiries, lest Menaechmus should contrive to baulk him of his banquet altogether.

[13] My only eye: By this it appears that Peniculus has but one eye. In the Curculio, the Parasite of that name is also represented as having but one eye.

[14] Let consume this day: He supposes the day to be dead so far as business is concerned; the "coena," which generally commenced about three o'clock in the afternoon (and sometimes, perhaps, the "prandium" as well), was followed by "potatio" or "drinking," which by such characters as Menaechmus and the Parasite would

be prolonged to midnight, when they would see the day dead, and celebrate its funeral in their orgies.

[15] To its navel: "Umbilicus," the "navel," was a term much used to signify the middle part of anything. Thus Delphi was called the "umbilicus," or "navel," of the world.

[16] An excellent charioteer: The drivers of the chariots at the Circensian games were called "agitatores." Of course they would look back every now, and then to see how near their opponents were, that they might keep the lead.

[17] You've removed: Peniculus now loses patience, and reflects that there is many a slip between the cup and the lip.

[18] Supernumeraries: The "adscriptivi," who were also called "accensi," were a body of reserve troops who followed the Roman army without any military duties to perform, and who were drafted off to supply the deficiencies in the legions. In battle they were placed in the rear of the army. Of course they could not claim the same advantages as the regular soldier; and his own position is likened by the Parasite to theirs.

[19] A spoil from: "Exuviae" means either the slough or cast skin of a snake, or the spoil taken from the enemy. Perhaps the latter is the sense in which it is here meant, as he has described his operations as a perfect campaign.

[20] With your teething him: Judging from this remark, perhaps she has accidentally forgotten to kiss her dupe, Menaechmus.

[21] From Hippolyta: Hercules was commanded by Eurystheus to obtain the belt or girdle of Hippolyta, or Antiope, the Queen of the Amazons. This he effected, and gave her in marriage to his companion Theseus, by whom, after giving birth to Hippolytus, she was put to death. Some accounts, however, state that she was slain by Hercules.

[22] Bacon off the gammon: He facetiously calls bacon "pernonides," literally, "the son of the gammon."

[23] Duty of eight persons: Athenaeus, Book I., quotes a passage from Eubulus, the Comic writer, where he represents a Parasite as being counted or two or even three at table.

ACT II.

SCENE I.

Enter MENAECHMUS SOSICLES *and* MESSENIO.

MENAECHMUS SOSICLES. There's no greater pleasure to voyagers, in my notion, Messenio, than at the moment when from sea they espy the land afar.

MESSENIO. There is a greater, I'll say it without subterfuge,—if on your arrival you see the land that is your own. But, prithee, why are we now come to Epidamnus? Why, like the sea, are we going round all the islands?

MENAECHMUS SOSICLES. To seek for my own twin-brother born?

MESSENIO. Why, what end is there to be of searching for him? This is the sixth year that we've devoted our attention to this business. We have been already carried round the Istrians [1], the Hispanians, the Massilians, the Illyrians, all the Upper Adriatic Sea, and foreign Greece [2], and all the shores of Italy, wherever the sea reaches them. If you had been searching for a needle, I do believe you would, long ere this, have found the needle, if it were visible. Among the living are we seeking a person that's dead; for long ago should we have found him if he had been alive.

MENAECHMUS SOSICLES. For that reason I am looking for a person to give me that information for certain, who can say that he knows that he really is dead; after that I shall never take any trouble in seeking further. But otherwise I shall never, while I'm alive, desist; I know how dear he is to my heart.

MESSENIO. You are seeking a knot in a bulrush [3]. Why don't we return homeward hence, unless we are to write a history? [4]

MENAECHMUS SOSICLES. Have done with your witty sayings, and be on your guard against a mischief. Don't you be troublesome; this matter shan't be done at your bidding.

MESSENIO. (*aside*). Aye, aye; by that same expression do I rest assured that I'm a slave; he couldn't in a few words have said more in a plain-spoken way. But still I can't restrain myself from speaking. (*Aloud*.) Do you hear, Menaechmus? When I look in the purse, I find, i' faith, we're only equipped for our journey like summer travellers [5]. By my troth, I guess, if you don't be returning home, while you're seeking your twin-brother, you'll surely be groaning [6], when you have nothing left. For such is this race of people; among the men of Epidamnus there are debauchees and very great drinkers; swindlers besides, and many wheedlers are living in this city; then the women in the harlot line are said nowhere in the world to be more captivating. The name of Epidamnus was given to this city for the very reason, because hardly any person sojourns here without some damnable mishaps [7].

MENAECHMUS SOSICLES. I'll guard against that. Just give me the purse this way.

MESSENIO. What do you want with it?

MENAECHMUS SOSICLES. I'm apprehensive then about yourself, from your expressions.

MESSENIO. Why are you apprehensive?

MENAECHMUS SOSICLES. Lest you should cause me some damnable mishap in Epidamnus. You are a great admirer of the women, Messenio, and I'm a passionate man, of an unmanageable disposition; of both these things will I have a care, when I've got the money, that you shall not commit a fault, and that I shall not be in a passion with you.

MESSENIO. (*giving him the purse*). Take and keep it; with all my heart you may do so.

SCENE II.

Enter CYLINDRUS, *with a basket of provisions.*

CYLINDRUS. I've catered well, and to my mind. I'll set a good breakfast before the breakfasters. But see, I perceive Menaechmus. Woe to my back; the guests are now already walking before the door, before I've returned with the provisions. I'll go and accost him. Save you, Menaechmus.

MENAECHMUS SOSICLES. The Gods bless you, whoever you are. * * * * *

CYLINDRUS. * * * * * who I am?

MESSENIO. I' faith, not I, indeed.

CYLINDRUS. Where are the other guests?

MENAECHMUS SOSICLES. What guests are you enquiring about?

CYLINDRUS. Your Parasite.

MENAECHMUS SOSICLES. My Parasite? Surely this fellow's deranged.

MESSENIO. Didn't I tell you that there were many swindlers here?

MENAECHMUS SOSICLES. What Parasite of mine, young man, are you enquiring about?

CYLINDRUS. Peniculus.

MENAECHMUS SOSICLES. * * * * * Where is my * * * * *?

MESSENIO. See, I've got your sponge [8] [*Peniculus*] all safe in the wallet.

CYLINDRUS. Menaechmus, you've come here too soon for breakfast; I'm but now returning with the provisions.

MENAECHMUS SOSICLES. Answer me this, young man: at what price do pigs sell here [9], unblemished ones, for sacrifice?

CYLINDRUS. At a didrachm a-piece.

MENAECHMUS SOSICLES. (*holding out his hand*). Receive, then, a didrachm of me; bid a sacrifice be made for you at my expense; for, by my faith, I really am sure in very truth that you are deranged, who are annoying me, a person that's a stranger, whoever you are.

CYLINDRUS. I am Cylindrus; don't you know my name?

MENAECHMUS SOSICLES. Whether you are Cylindrus or Caliendrus [10], confound you. I don't know you, and, in fact, I don't want to know you.

CYLINDRUS. Well, your name, however, is Menaechmus, that I do know.

MENAECHMUS SOSICLES. You speak like a sane person when you call me by my name. But where have you known me?

CYLINDRUS. Where have I known you, you who have Erotium, this mistress of mine (*pointing to the house*), for your lady?

MENAECHMUS SOSICLES. By my troth, I have not, nor do I know yourself what person you are.

CYLINDRUS. Not know who I am, who have many a time filled the cups for your own self at our house, when you've been drinking?

MESSENIO. Woe to me, that I've got nothing with which to break this fellow's head.

MENAECHMUS SOSICLES. Are you in the habit of filling the cups for me, who, before this day, have never beheld Epidamnus, nor been there?

CYLINDRUS. Do you deny it?

MENAECHMUS SOSICLES. Upon my honor, I decidedly do deny it.

CYLINDRUS. Don't you live in that house? (*Pointing to the house of* MENAECHMUS *of Epidamnus*.)

MENAECHMUS SOSICLES. May the Gods send to perdition those that live there.

CYLINDRUS. Surely, this fellow's mad, who is thus uttering curses against his own self. Do you hear, Menaechmus?

MENAECHMUS SOSICLES. What do you want?

CYLINDRUS. If you take my advice, that didrachm, which you just now promised to give me—you would order, if you were wise, a pig to be procured with it for yourself. For, i' faith, you really for sure are not in your senses, Menaechmus, who are now uttering curses against your own self.

MENAECHMUS SOSICLES. Alas! By my faith, a very silly fellow, and an annoyance to me.

CYLINDRUS. (*to* MESSENIO). He's in the habit of often joking with me in this fashion. How very droll he is, when his wife isn't present. How say you——?

MENAECHMUS SOSICLES. What do you mean, you rascal?

CYLINDRUS. (*pointing to the basket*). Has this that you see been provided in sufficient quantity for three persons, or am I to provide still more for yourself and the Parasite and the lady?

MENAECHMUS SOSICLES. What ladies—what Parasites are you talking about?

MESSENIO. What, you villain, urges you to be an annoyance to him?

CYLINDRUS. Pray what business have you with me? I don't know you; I'm talking to this person, whom I do know.

MENAECHMUS SOSICLES. By my troth, you are not a person in his right senses, that I know for sure.

CYLINDRUS. I'll have these things cooked directly; there shall be no delay. Don't you be going after this anywhere at a distance from the house. Do you want anything?

MENAECHMUS SOSICLES. You to go to utter and extreme perdition.

CYLINDRUS. I' faith, 'twere better for you to go in-doors at once and take your place, while I'm subjecting these things to the strength of the fire [11]. I'll go in-doors now, and tell Erotium that you are standing here, that she may fetch you away hence, rather than you be standing here out of doors. (*He goes into the house.*)

SCENE III.

MENAECHMUS SOSICLES. Is he gone then? He is gone. By my faith, I find by experience that your words are not untrue.

MESSENIO. Do you only be on your guard; for I do believe that some woman in the harlot line is living here, as, in fact. this madman said, who has just gone away from here.

MENAECHMUS SOSICLES. But I wonder how he came to know my name.

MESSENIO. I' faith, 'tis far from surprising: courtesans have this custom; they send servant-boys and servant-girls down to the harbour; if any foreign ship comes into port, they enquire of what country it is, and what its name is; after that, at once they set themselves to work, and fasten themselves upon him; if they inveigle him, they send him home a ruined man. Now in this harbour there stands a piratical craft, against which I really think that we must be on our guard.

MENAECHMUS SOSICLES. I' troth, you really counsel aright.

MESSENIO. Then, in fine, shall I be sure that I've counselled aright, if you are rightly on your guard.

MENAECHMUS SOSICLES. Be silent for a moment, then; for the door makes a noise. Let's see who's coming out from there.

MESSENIO. Meanwhile, I'll lay this down. (*He puts down the wallet.*) Do you keep watch upon these things, if you please, you sailors [12].

SCENE IV.

Enter EROTIUM *from her house.*

EROTIUM. (*speaking to her* SERVANTS *within*). Leave the door ajar [13] thus; begone. I don't want it shut: prepare, attend, and provide within; what is requisite, let it be done. Lay down the couches, burn the perfumes; neatness, that is the charm for the minds of lovers. Our agreeableness is for the lover's loss, for our own gain. (*To herself.*) But where is he whom the Cook said was in front of the house? O, I see him there—one who is of service to me, and who profits me very much. And right willingly is such usage shown to him, as he deserves to be of especial importance in my house. Now I'll accost him; I'll address him of my own accord. (*To* MENAECHMUS.) My dear life, it seems wonderful to me that you are standing here out of doors, for whom the door is wide open, more so than your own house, inasmuch as this house is at your service. Everything's ready as you requested and as you desired; nor have you now any delay in-doors. The breakfast, as you ordered, is prepared here; when you please, you may go and take your place.

MENAECHMUS SOSICLES. To whom is this woman addressing herself?

EROTIUM. Why, I'm talking to yourself.

MENAECHMUS SOSICLES. What business have I ever had with you, or have I now?

EROTIUM. Troth, inasmuch as Venus has willed that you singly above all I should exalt; and that not without your deserving it. For, by my faith, you alone make me, by your kindnesses, to be thriving.

MENAECHMUS SOSICLES. For sure this woman is either mad or drunk, Messenio, that addresses me, a person whom she knows not in so familiar a way.

MESSENIO. Didn't I say that these things are in the habit of occurring here? The leaves are falling now; in comparison with this, if we shall be here for three days, the trees will be tumbling upon you.

For to such a degree are all these Courtesans wheedlers out of one's money. But only let me address her. Harkye, woman, I'm speaking to you.

EROTIUM. What's the matter?

MESSENIO. Where have you yourself known this person?

EROTIUM. In that same place where he has known me for this long time, in Epidamnus.

MESSENIO. In Epidamnus? A man who, until this day, has never put a foot here inside of this city.

EROTIUM. Heyday! You are making fun, my dear Menaechmus. But, prithee, why not go in? There, it will be more suitable for you.

MENAECHMUS SOSICLES. I' faith, this woman really does address me rightly by my name. I wonder very much what's the meaning of this business.

MESSENIO. (*aside*). That purse that you are carrying has been smelt out by her.

MENAECHMUS SOSICLES. (*aside*). I' faith, and rightly have you put me in mind. Take it, then; I'll know now whether she loves myself or the purse most. (*Gives him the purse.*)

EROTIUM. Let's go in the house to breakfast.

MENAECHMUS SOSICLES. You invite me kindly; so far, my thanks.

EROTIUM. Why then did you bid me a while since prepare a breakfast for you?

MENAECHMUS SOSICLES. I, bid you prepare?

EROTIUM. Certainly you did, for yourself and your Parasite.

MENAECHMUS SOSICLES. A plague, what Parasite? Surely this woman isn't quite right in her senses.

EROTIUM. Peniculus.

MENAECHMUS SOSICLES. Who is this Peniculus The one with which the shoes are wiped clean? [14]

EROTIUM. Him, I mean, who came with you a while ago, when you brought me the mantle which you purloined from your wife.

MENAECHMUS SOSICLES. What do you mean? I, gave you a mantle, which I purloined from my wife? Are you in your senses? Surely this woman dreams standing, after the manner of a gelding. [15]

EROTIUM. Why does it please you to hold me in ridicule, and to deny to me things that have been done by you?

MENAECHMUS SOSICLES. Tell me what it is that I deny after having done it?

EROTIUM. That you to-day gave me your wife's mantle.

MENAECHMUS SOSICLES. Even still do I deny it. Indeed, I never had a wife, nor have I one; nor have I ever set my foot here within the city gate since I was born. I breakfasted on board ship; thence did I come this way, and here I met you.

EROTIUM. See that now; I'm undone, wretched creature that I am! What ship are you now telling me about?

MENAECHMUS SOSICLES. A wooden one, weather-beaten full oft, cracked full oft, many a time thumped with mallets. Just as the implements of the furrier [16]; so peg is close to peg.

EROTIUM. Now, prithee, do leave off making fun of me, and step this way with me.

MENAECHMUS SOSICLES. * * * * * for, madam, you are looking for some other person, I know not whom, not me.

EROTIUM. Don't I know you, Menaechmus, the son of your father Moschus, who are said to have been born in Sicily, at Syracuse, where King Agathocles reigned, and after him Pintia [17], the third

Liparo, who at his death left the kingdom to Hiero—which Hiero is now king?

MENAECHMUS SOSICLES. You say, madam, what is not untrue.

MESSENIO. By Jupiter, hasn't this woman come from there, who knows you so readily? * * * * *

MENAECHMUS SOSICLES. (*apart*). Troth, I think she must not be denied.

MESSENIO. (*apart*). Don't you do it. You are undone, if you enter inside her threshold.

MENAECHMUS SOSICLES. (*apart*). But you only hold your tongue * * * * * The matter goes on well. I shall assent to the woman, whatever she shall say, if I can get some entertainment. Just now, madam (*speaking to her in a low voice*), I contradicted you not undesignedly; I was afraid of that fellow, lest he might carry word to my wife about the mantle and the breakfast. Now, when you please, let's go in-doors.

EROTIUM. Are you going to wait for the Parasite as well?

MENAECHMUS SOSICLES. I'm neither going to wait for him, nor do I care a straw for him, nor, if he should come, do I want him to be admitted in-doors.

EROTIUM. By my faith, I shall do that not at all reluctantly. But do you know what I beg you to do?

MENAECHMUS SOSICLES. Only command me what you will.

EROTIUM. For you to take that mantle which you gave me just now to the embroiderer's [18], that it may be trimmed again, and that some work may be added which I want.

MENAECHMUS SOSICLES. I' faith, you say what's right; in such a way shall it be disguised that my wife shan't know that you are wearing it, if she should see you in the street.

EROTIUM. Then take it away with you just now, when you go away.

MENAECHMUS SOSICLES. By all means.

EROTIUM. Let's go in-doors. (*Goes into her house.*)

MENAECHMUS SOSICLES. I'll follow you this instant; I only wish to speak to this person. So, there! Messenio, step to me this way.

MESSENIO. What's the matter?

MENAECHMUS SOSICLES. Listen.

MESSENIO. What need for it?

MENAECHMUS SOSICLES. There is need, I know what you'll say to me——

MESSENIO. So much the worse.

MENAECHMUS SOSICLES. Hold your tongue * * * * * I've got some spoil; thus much of the business have I begun upon. Go, and, as quick as you can, take away those peoples [19] at once to an inn [20]. Then do you take care to come and meet me [21] before sunset.

MESSENIO. Don't you know that these people are harlots, master?

MENAECHMUS SOSICLES. Hold your tongue, I say, and go you away from here. It will cost me pain, not you, if I do anything here that's foolish. This woman is silly and inexperienced. So far as I've perceived just now, there's some spoil for us here. (*He goes into the house of* EROTIUM.)

MESSENIO. I'm undone. Are you going away then? He is certainly ruined; the piratical craft is now leading the boat straight to destruction. But I'm an unreasonable fellow to wish to rule my master; he bought me to obey his orders, not to be his commander. (*To the* ATTENDANTS.) Follow me, that, as I'm ordered, I may come in good time to meet my master.

FOOTNOTES TO ACT II.

[1] The Istrians: The Istrians were a people of the north of Italy, near the Adriatic Sea, and adjoining to Illyricum. The Illyrians inhabited the countries now called Dalmatia and Sclavonia. The Massilians were the natives of the city of Massilia, now called Marseilles, in the south of France, where Pontius Pilate ended his days in banishment. The Hispani were the inhabitants of Hispania, now Spain.

[2] And foreign Greece: The "Graecia exotica," or "foreign Greece," here mentioned, was the southern part of Italy, which was also called "Magna Graecia," in consequence of the great number of Grecian settlements there. The Greeks were in the habit of calling the Sicilians and Calabrians *Hellênas exôtikous*, "barbarian" or "foreign Greeks."

[3] In a bulrush: Those who made difficulties when there really was no difficulty at all, were said "in scirpo nodum quaerere" "to seek a knot in a bulrush," the stem of which is perfectly smooth.

[4] To write a history: A narrative or history of their travels. Boxhorn thinks that the remark alludes to the voyage of Ulysses, a counterpart of which voyage could not be written without great personal observation, and an extensive knowledge of geography.

[5] Like summer travellers: Of course lighter garments and a less weight of luggage would be carried by travellers in the heat of summer.

[6] You'll surely be groaning: He intends a puerile play upon the resemblance of the words "gemes," "will be groaning," and "geminum," "twin-brother."

[7] Some damnable mishap: "Sine damno," Literally, "without mischief" or "mishap." He puns on the resemblance of "damnum" to "Epidamnum." An attempt has been made in the translation to preserve the resemblance in some degree.

[8] I've got your sponge: Menaechmus takes Cylindrus to mean as though he were really talking about a "peniculus," or "sponge,"

used for the purposes of a napkin. He turns to Messenio, and probably says (in the mutilated passage), "Where is my peniculus?" on which the servant, taking it out of the "vidulus," or travelling-bag. says, "Here it is, quite safe."

[9] Do pigs sell here: Pigs without blemish were sacrificed to the Lares, or household Gods, in behalf of those who were afflicted with insanity. Menaechmus Sosicles adopts this as a quiet way of telling Cylindrus that he must be mad.

[10] Cylindrus or Caliendrus: Probably Cylindrus is so called from the words "cylindrus," "a cylinder," in the sense of a "rolling-pin." Sosicles plays upon its resemblance to "caliendrus," which perhaps meant a "peruke" or "wig," as the Latin word "caliendrum" had that signification.

[11] Strength of the fire: Vulcani ad violentiam. Literally "to the violence of Vulcan," the God of fire.

[12] You sailors: Some Commentators think that by the words "navales pedes" he means "oars," as being the feet, or source of motion to the ship, and that Messenio puts his luggage upon some oars on the ground close by, telling them to be good enough to keep it all safe. It is more probable, however, that he is addressing some of the crew, perhaps the rowers who have carried the luggage from the ship. Others suggest that the luggage-porters, who awaited the arrival of ships with passengers and merchandize, are here referred to. This line, in Cotter's translation, is rendered, "Observe these things now, if you please. Behold the ship!" with this note, "Navales pedes, the oars of a ship, put for the ship itself."! De l'Oeuvre ingeniously suggests that "paedes" is the correct reading, and the word is the Greek *paides* Latinized, and signifying, in the present instance, the "ship-boys" or "servants."

[13] Leave the door ajar: Ladies of Erotium's character would find it more convenient to have their doors ajar, that persons might step in unperceived, besides, in the present instance, she wishes the "janitor" not to shut the door, as me expects to return directly with Menaechmus.

[14] Are wiped clean: "Baxae" or "baxeae" were sandals made a twigs or fibres. They were often worn on the stage by Comic actors, and

probably on saying this, Menaechmus Sosicles points to his own. The Egyptians made them of palm-leaves and papyrus. They were much worn by the philosophers of ancient times. Probably the "peniculi," made of the tails of oxen, were much used for the purpose of dusting shoes.

[15] Manner of a gelding: He compares her to a horse, which sleeps and dreams (if it dreams at all) in a standing posture.

[16] Of the furrier: The "pellio," "furrier" or "skinner," would require a great many pegs in fastening down the skins for the purpose of stretching them. Meursius thinks that Plautus intends a sly hit here at Pellio, the bad actor, who is mentioned in the Second Scene of the Second Act in the Bacchides. If so, the joke is quite lost on us.

[17] After him Pintia: She is supposed, by the Commentators, to be purposely represented here as quite mistaken in her historical facts, and as making nothing but a confused jumble of them. Some think that the words "Pintia" and "Liparo" are ablative cases; but it is much more probable that they are nominatives. Gronovius thinks that one Phintias is alluded to, who, as we are told by Diodorus Siculus, assumed the government at Agrigentum after the death of Agathocles. He did not, however, reign at Syracuse. We do not learn from history that Hiero received the government from Liparo, but, on the contrary, that his virtuous character was the sole ground for his election to the sovereignty. Lipara was the name of one of the Aeolian islands (now called the Isles of Lipari), not far from the coast of Sicily. Some think that she means to call Agathocles by the additional names of Plintias (and not Pintia) from *plintos*, "pottery," as he had exercised the trade of a potter, and of "Liparo," from the Greek *lupêros*, "savage," by reason of the cruelty of which he was guilty in the latter part of his life. This notion seems, however, to be more fanciful than well-founded.

[18] To the embroiderer's: "Phrygionem." As the natives of Phrygia were very dexterous at embroidering, and their services were much sought for the purposes of luxury, all embroiderers, in time came to be called "phrygiones." Cotter renders "ad phrygionem" here "to Phrygia," and so throughout the whole play!

[19] Those people: By "istos" he probably means the sailors or porters who were carrying the luggage.

[20] To an inn: The accommodation of the "taberna diversoria," or "diversorium," was generally of a humble kind, and these places were mostly adapted for the poorer classes only.

[21] Come and meet me: That is, as his "adversitor," which was the title given to the servant whose duty it was to fetch his master home in the evening.

ACT III.

SCENE I.

Enter PENICULUS.

PENICULUS. More than thirty years have I been born yet during that time I never did any more mischievous or more evil trick than this day, when, to my misfortune, I thrust myself into the midst of the assembly [1]. while I was gaping about there, Menaechmus stole away from me, and went, I suppose, to his mistress, and didn't want to take me. May all the Divinities confound that man who first mischievously devised the holding of an assembly, which keeps men thus engaged. By my troth, is it not fitting that men who are disengaged should be chosen for that purpose? These, when they are cited, if they are not present, let the officers exact the fine [2] forthwith * * * * * the senate * * * * * Abundance of men are there who every day eat their victuals alone, who have no business, who are neither invited nor invite to feast; these ought to give their attendance at the assembly and the law-courts [3]. If so it had been, this say I shouldn't have lost my breakfast; to which I deemed myself as much accustomed, as to see myself alive. I'll go; even yet the hope of the scraps comforts my mind. But why do I see Menaechmus here? He's coming out of doors with a chaplet on? The banquet is removed; i' faith, I come just in time to meet him. I'll watch the fellow, what he's about, then I'll go and accost him. (*He steps aside.*)

SCENE II.

Enter MENAECHMUS SOSICLES, *from the house of* EROTIUM, *with the mantle on.*

MENAECHMUS SOSICLES. (*speaking to* EROTIUM *within*). Can't you rest content, if this day I bring it you back in good time, nicely and properly trimmed? I'll cause you to say it isn't itself, so much shall it be disguised.

PENICULUS. (*apart*). He's carrying the mantle to the embroiderer's, the breakfast finished and the wine drunk up, and the Parasite shut out of doors. By my troth, I'm not the person that I am, if I don't handsomely avenge this injury and myself. 'Tis requisite I should watch * * * * * I'll give something.

MENAECHMUS SOSICLES. (*to himself*). O ye immortal Gods! on what man ever have you conferred more blessings in one day, who hoped for less? I've been breakfasting, drinking, feasting with a mistress; and I've carried off this mantle, of which she shall no more be owner after this day.

PENICULUS. Isn't he now talking about me, and my share of the repast? I can't well hear what he says.

MENAECHMUS SOSICLES. (*to himself*). She says that I secretly gave her this, and that I stole it away from my wife. When I perceived that she was mistaken, at once I began to assent, as though I really had had acquaintanceship with her. Whatever the woman said, the same said I. What need of many words? I was never entertained at less expense.

PENICULUS. (*apart*). I'll accost the fellow; for I quite long to have a row.

MENAECHMUS SOSICLES. Who's this that's coming up towards me? (*Takes off the mantle, and hides it.*)

PENICULUS. What say you, you fellow lighter than a feather, most rascally and most abandoned—you disgraceful man—you cheat, and most worthless fellow? Why have I deserved this of you? For what reason should you ruin me? How you stole yourself away from me just now at the Forum. You've been performing the funeral of the breakfast in my absence. Why did you dare to do so, when I was entitled to it in an equal degree?

MENAECHMUS SOSICLES. Young man, prithee, what business with me have you, who are thus purposely insulting a person whom you know not? Do you wish a punishment to be given you for your abuse?

PENICULUS. Do be quiet; by my faith, I discover that you've done that already indeed.

MENAECHMUS SOSICLES. Answer me, young man, I beg; what is your name?

PENICULUS. Are you laughing at me, as well, as though you didn't know my name?

MENAECHMUS SOSICLES. By my troth, I never saw or knew you, that I'm aware of, before this day; but at all events, whoever you are, if you do what's right, you won't be an annoyance to me.

PENICULUS. Don't you know me?

MENAECHMUS SOSICLES. I shouldn't deny it if I did know you.

PENICULUS. Menaechmus, awake.

MENAECHMUS SOSICLES. I' troth, I really am awake, so far as I know.

PENICULUS. Don't you know your own Parasite?

MENAECHMUS SOSICLES. Young man, I find that your headpiece isn't sound.

PENICULUS. Answer me; have you not purloined that mantle from your wife to-day, and given it to Erotium?

MENAECHMUS SOSICLES. I' faith I have no wife, nor have I given the mantle to Erotium, nor have I purloined it.

PENICULUS. Are you really in your senses? * * * * * This matter's settled [4]. Did I not see you coming out of doors clad in a mantle?

MENAECHMUS SOSICLES. Woe to your head. Do you think that all people are effeminate rogues [5] because you are one? Do you declare that I was clothed in a mantle?

PENICULUS. Troth, I really do.

MENAECHMUS SOSICLES. Why don't you go where you are deserving to go, or else request yourself to be atoned for, you downright madman?

PENICULUS. By my troth, never shall any one prevail upon me not to tell your wife the whole matter now, just as it happened. All these insults shall be retorted upon yourself. I'll take care that you shan't have devoured the breakfast unpunished. (*He goes into the house of* MENAECHMUS *of Epidamnus*.)

MENAECHMUS SOSICLES. What's the meaning of this business? Why, Just as I see each person, do they all make fun of me in this way? But the door makes a noise.

SCENE III.

Enter a MAID-SERVANT, *from the house of* EROTIUM.

MAID-SERVANT of Erotium. Menaechmus, Erotium says that she entreats you much, that at the same opportunity you'll take this to the goldsmith's, and add to it an ounce in weight of gold, and order the bracelet [6] to be fashioned anew. (*Gives him a bracelet.*)

MENAECHMUS SOSICLES. Tell her that I'll attend both to this and anything else that she shall wish, if she wishes anything else attended to.

MAID-SERVANT of Erotium. Do you know what this bracelet is?

MENAECHMUS SOSICLES. I don't know, unless it's of gold.

MAID-SERVANT of Erotium. This is the same one that you once said that you had secretly stolen out of the closet from your wife.

MENAECHMUS SOSICLES. By my troth, 'twas never done.

MAID-SERVANT of Erotium. Prithee, don't you remember it?

MENAECHMUS SOSICLES. Not in the least.

MAID-SERVANT of Erotium. Give it me back then, if you don't remember it. (*Tries to take it.*)

MENAECHMUS SOSICLES. Stop. (*Pretends to examine the bracelet.*) O yes, I really do remember it; it's the same, I believe, that I presented to her.

MAID-SERVANT of Erotium. I' faith, it is the same.

MENAECHMUS SOSICLES. Where are the clasps which I gave her together with them?

MAID-SERVANT of Erotium. You never gave her any.

MENAECHMUS SOSICLES. Why, faith, I gave them together with this * * * * *

MAID-SERVANT of Erotium. Shall I say that you'll attend to it?

MENAECHMUS SOSICLES. Do say so; it shall be attended to. I'll take care that the mantle and the bracelet are brought back together.

MAID-SERVANT of Erotium. My dear Menaechmus, do, pray, give me some earrings [7], the pendants to be made two didrachms in weight; that I may look on you with delight when you come to our house.

MENAECHMUS SOSICLES. Be it so. Give me the gold [8]; I'll find the price of the workmanship.

MAID-SERVANT of Erotium. Give it yourself, please; at a future time I'll give it you back.

MENAECHMUS SOSICLES. No, give it yourself; at a future time I'll give it you twofold.

MAID-SERVANT of Erotium. I haven't any.

MENAECHMUS SOSICLES. But when you have it, do you give it me, then.

MAID-SERVANT of Erotium. Do you wish for aught?

MENAECHMUS SOSICLES. Say that I'll attend to these things, (*aside*) to be sold as soon as they can, and for what they'll fetch. (*The* MAID-SERVANT *goes into the house.*) Has she now gone off in-doors? She's gone, and has shut the door. Surely all the Gods are favouring, amplifying, and prospering me. But why do I delay while opportunity and time are granted me to get away from these procurers' dens? Make haste, Menaechmus; pull foot and quicken your pace. I'll take off this chaplet [9], and throw it away on the left hand side (*throws the chaplet down*), that, if they follow me, they may think I've gone in that direction. I'll go and meet my servant, if I can, that he may learn from me these blessings which the Gods confer upon me.

FOOTNOTES TO ACT III.

[1] Midst of the assembly: This "concio" was the sitting of the court for the trial of causes, to which we shall find further reference in the sequel, when it is explained how he happened to lose sight of Menaechmus.

[2] Exact the fine: He suggests that Menaechmus has possibly been summoned, in his capacity as a citizen, to the "concio," for the purpose of being present at the trials going on. The Parasite curses this custom, and wishes that they would summon only the idle men, and not those engaged in the important business of feasting their friends. There is some doubt as to the meaning of "census capiant," but it probably signifies "let them exact the fine."

[3] And the law-courts: The "comitia" of the Romans have been referred to in a previous Note.

[4] This matter's settled: "Occisa est haec res." Literally, "this matter is killed;" somewhat similar to our expression, "the murder is out."

[5] Effeminate rogues: "Cinaedos." Literally, "dancers" or "dancing-masters," who, being effeminate persons, would be more likely to wear a "palla" of gay colours. [The translator is suppressing the actual meaning of the word. A *cinaedus* (Greek *kinaidos*) is a homosexual man.]

[6] Order the bracelet: "Spinter" or "spinther" is another name, derived from the Greek *sphinktêr*, for the Latin "armilla" or bracelet. It received its Greek name, from its keeping in its place by compressing the arm of the wearer. Festus tells us that the bracelet called "spinter" was worn by the Roman ladies on the left arm, while the "armilla" was worn on either.

[7] Give me some earrings: The drops of the earrings were probably to be of the weight of two didrachms. The earring was called among the Romans "inauris," and by the Greeks *enôtion*. The Greeks also called it *ellobion*, from its being inserted in the lobe of the ear. These ornaments were worn by both sexes among the Lydians, Persians, Libyans, Carthaginians, and other nations. Among the Greeks and Romans, the females alone were in the habit of

wearing them. As with us, the earring consisted of a ring, and a drop, called "stalagmium," the ring being generally of gold, though bronze was sometimes used by the common people. Pearls, especially those of elongated form, called "elenchi," were very much valued for pendants.

[8] Give me the gold: He asks for the gold with the intention of stealing it; for, in spite of their wealth, it is evident, from this, and what appears in the sequel, that both he and his brother are by nature arrant thieves.

[9] Take off this chaplet: This he had been wearing at the "prandium," or "breakfast," at Erotium's house. The latter appears to be a more fitting name for a meal that was taken generally about twelve o'clock; while "the coena," which commenced in general at about three, cannot with propriety be termed anything else than a "dinner."

ACT IV.

SCENE I.

Enter, from her house, the WIFE *of* MENAECHMUS *of Epidamnus, followed by* PENICULUS.

THE WIFE OF MENAECHMUS of Epidamnus. And shall I allow myself to remain in wedlock [1] here, when my husband secretly pilfers whatever's in the house, and carries it thence off to his mistress?

PENICULUS. Why don't you hold your peace? I'll let you now catch him in the fact; do you only follow me this way. (They go to the opposite side of the stage.) In a state of drunkenness, with a chaplet on, he was carrying the mantle to the embroiderer's, which he purloined from you at home to-day. But see, here is the chaplet which he had on. (Seeing the chaplet on the ground.) Now am I saying false? Aha, this way has he gone, if you wish to trace his footsteps. And, by my faith, see, here he comes on his way back most opportunely, but he isn't wearing the mantle.

THE WIFE OF MENAECHMUS of Epidamnus. What now shall I do to him?

PENICULUS. The same as usual; abuse him.

THE WIFE OF MENAECHMUS of Epidamnus. So I am resolved.

PENICULUS. Let's step aside this way watch him from ambush. (*They retire on one side.*)

SCENE II.

Enter MENAECHMUS *of Epidamnus.*

MENAECHMUS of Epidamnus. (*to himself*). How we do practise a custom here that is very foolish and extremely troublesome, and how even those who are the most worthy and great [2] do follow this habit: all wish their dependants to be many in number; whether they are deserving or undeserving, about that they don't enquire. Their property is more enquired about, than what the reputation of their clients is for honor. If any person is poor and not dishonest, he is considered worthless; but if a rich man is dishonest, he is considered a good client. Those who neither regard laws nor any good or justice at all, the same have zealous patrons. What has been entrusted to them, they deny to have been so entrusted; men full of litigation, rapacious, and fraudulent; who have acquired their property either by usury or by perjury; their whole pleasure is in litigation. When the day for trial is appointed, at the same time it is mentioned to their patrons, in order that they may plead for them, about what they have done amiss. Before the people [3], or at law before the Praetor, or before the Aedile, is the cause tried. Just so, this day, a certain dependant has kept me very much engaged, nor was it allowed me to do what I wished, or in company with whom I wished; so fast did he stick to me, so much did he detain me. Before the Aedile, in behalf of his doings, very many and very disgraceful, did I plead his cause; a compromise I obtained, obscure and perplexed—more than enough I said, and than I needed to say, that surety for him [4] might end this litigation. What did he do? Well, what? He gave bail. And never did I at any time see any person more clearly detected; three very adverse witnesses against all his misdeeds were there. May all the Gods confound him, he has so spoilt this day for me; and myself as well, who ever this day beheld the Forum with my eyes. I ordered a breakfast to be prepared; my mistress is expecting me, I'm sure; as soon as ever I had the opportunity, I made haste immediately to leave the Forum. Now, I suppose, she's angry with me; the mantle, however, will appease her that I gave her, the one I took away to-day from my wife and carried to Erotium here.

PENICULUS. (*apart to the* WIFE). What say you now?

THE WIFE OF MENAECHMUS of Epidamnus. (*apart*). That I'm unfortunately married to a worthless fellow.

PENICULUS. (*apart*). Do you perfectly hear what he says?

THE WIFE OF MENAECHMUS of Epidamnus. (*apart*). Quite well.

MENAECHMUS of Epidamnus. If I am wise, I shall be going hence in-doors, where it may be comfortable for me.

PENICULUS. (*coming forward*) Stop; on the contrary, it shall be uncomfortable.

MENAECHMUS of Epidamnus. * * * * * she is very sorrowful; this doesn't quite please me, but I'll speak to her. Tell me, my wife, what is it amiss with you?

PENICULUS. (*to the* WIFE). The pretty fellow's soothing you.

MENAECHMUS of Epidamnus. Can't you cease being annoying to me? Did I address you?

THE WIFE OF MENAECHMUS of Epidamnus. (*turning away from* MENAECHMUS). Take yourself off—away with your caresses from me. Do you persist in it?

MENAECHMUS of Epidamnus. Why are you offended with me?

THE WIFE OF MENAECHMUS of Epidamnus. You ought to know.

PENICULUS. The rascal knows, but he pretends not to know.

MENAECHMUS of Epidamnus. Has any one of the servants done amiss? Do either the maid or the men-servants give you saucy answers? Speak out; it shan't be done with impunity.

THE WIFE OF MENAECHMUS of Epidamnus. You are trifling.

MENAECHMUS of Epidamnus. Surely you are angry at some one of the domestics?

THE WIFE OF MENAECHMUS of Epidamnus. You are trifling.

MENAECHMUS of Epidamnus. Are you angry with me at all events?

THE WIFE OF MENAECHMUS of Epidamnus. Now you are not trifling.

MENAECHMUS of Epidamnus. I' faith, I haven't done wrong in anything.

THE WIFE OF MENAECHMUS of Epidamnus. Ah! now you are trifling again.

MENAECHMUS of Epidamnus. Wife, what's the matter?

THE WIFE OF MENAECHMUS of Epidamnus. Do you ask me that?

MENAECHMUS of Epidamnus. Do you wish me to ask him? (*To* PENICULUS.) What's the matter?

THE WIFE OF MENAECHMUS of Epidamnus. The mantle.

MENAECHMUS of Epidamnus. The mantle?

THE WIFE OF MENAECHMUS of Epidamnus. A certain person has taken a mantle. (MENAECHMUS *starts*.)

PENICULUS. (to MENAECHMUS). Why are you alarmed?

MENAECHMUS of Epidamnus. For my part, I'm not alarmed at all— (*aside*) except about one thing; the mantle makes [5] my face mantle.

PENICULUS. (*aside to* MENAECHMUS). But as for me, you shouldn't have slily devoured the breakfast. (*To the* WIFE.) Go on against your husband.

MENAECHMUS of Epidamnus. (*making signs to* PENICULUS) . Won't you hold your tongue?

PENICULUS. Faith, I really will not hold my tongue. (*To the* WIFE.) He's nodding to me not to speak.

MENAECHMUS of Epidamnus. On my word, I really never did nod to you, or wink in any way.

PENICULUS. Nothing is more audacious than this man, who resolutely denies those things which you see.

MENAECHMUS of Epidamnus. By Jupiter and all the Gods, I swear, wife, that I did not nod to him; isn't that enough for you?

PENICULUS. She now believes you about that matter; go back again there.

MENAECHMUS of Epidamnus. Go back where?

PENICULUS. Why, to the embroiderer, as I suppose. Go and bring the mantle back.

MENAECHMUS of Epidamnus. What mantle is it?

PENICULUS. Now I hold my tongue, since he doesn't remember his own business.

THE WIFE OF MENAECHMUS of Epidamnus. Did you suppose that you could possibly commit these villanies unknown to me? By heavens, you have assuredly taken that away from me at a heavy usury; such is the return [6]. (*Shaking her fist.*)

PENICULUS. Such is the return. Do you make haste to eat up the breakfast in my absence; and then in your drunkenness make fun of me, with your chaplet on, before the house.

MENAECHMUS of Epidamnus. By all the powers, I have neither breakfasted, nor have I this day set foot inside of that house.

PENICULUS. Do you deny it?

MENAECHMUS of Epidamnus. By my troth, I really do deny it.

PENICULUS. Nothing is there more audacious than this fellow. Did I not just now see you standing here before the house, with a chaplet of flowers on, when you were declaring that my headpiece wasn't sound, and declaring that you didn't know me, and saying that you were a foreigner?

MENAECHMUS of Epidamnus. On the contrary, as some time since I parted with you, so I'm now returning home at last.

PENICULUS. I understand you. You didn't think it was in my power to take vengeance upon you; i' faith, I've told it all to your wife.

MENAECHMUS of Epidamnus. Told her what?

PENICULUS. I don't know; ask her own self.

MENAECHMUS of Epidamnus. (*turning to his* WIFE) . What's this, wife? Pray, what has he been telling you? What is it? Why are you silent? Why don't you say what it is?

THE WIFE OF MENAECHMUS of Epidamnus. As though you didn't know. I' faith, I certainly am a miserable woman.

MENAECHMUS of Epidamnus. Why are you a miserable woman? tell me.

THE WIFE OF MENAECHMUS of Epidamnus. Do you ask me?

MENAECHMUS of Epidamnus. Faith, I shouldn't ask you if I knew.

PENICULUS. O the wicked fellow; how he does dissemble. You cannot conceal it; she knows the matter thoroughly; by my faith, I've disclosed everything.

MENAECHMUS of Epidamnus. What is it?

THE WIFE OF MENAECHMUS of Epidamnus. Inasmuch as you are not at all ashamed, and don't wish to confess of your own accord, listen, and attend to this; I'll both let you know why I'm sorrowful, and what he has told me. My mantle has been purloined from me at home.

MENAECHMUS of Epidamnus. Mantle purloined from me?

PENICULUS. (*to the* WIFE) . D'you see how the rogue is catching you up? (*To* MENAECHMUS.) It was purloined from her, not from you; for certainly if it had been purloined from you, it would now be safe.

MENAECHMUS of Epidamnus. (*to* PENICULUS) . I've nothing to do with you. But (*to his* WIFE) what is it you say?

THE WIFE OF MENAECHMUS of Epidamnus. A mantle, I say, has been lost from home.

MENAECHMUS of Epidamnus. Who has stolen it?

THE WIFE OF MENAECHMUS of Epidamnus. I faith, he knows that, who took it away.

MENAECHMUS of Epidamnus. What person was it?

THE WIFE OF MENAECHMUS of Epidamnus. A certain Menaechmus.

MENAECHMUS of Epidamnus. By my troth, 'twas villainously done. Who is this Menaechmus?

THE WIFE OF MENAECHMUS of Epidamnus. You are he, I say.

MENAECHMUS of Epidamnus. I?

THE WIFE OF MENAECHMUS of Epidamnus. You.

MENAECHMUS of Epidamnus. Who accuses me?

THE WIFE OF MENAECHMUS of Epidamnus. I, myself.

PENICULUS. I, too; and you carried it off to Erotium here, your mistress.

MENAECHMUS of Epidamnus. I, gave it her?

PENICULUS. You, you, I say. Do you wish for an owl [7] to be brought here, to say "you, you," continually to you? For we are now quite tired of it.

MENAECHMUS of Epidamnus. By Jupiter and all the Gods, I swear, wife (and isn't that enough for you?), that I did not give it.

PENICULUS. Aye, and I, by all the powers, that we are telling no untruth.

MENAECHMUS of Epidamnus. But I haven't given it away, but just only lent it to be made use of.

THE WIFE OF MENAECHMUS of Epidamnus. But, i' faith, for my part, I don't lend either your scarf or your cloak out of the house, to any one, to be made use of. 'Tis fair that the woman should lend out of the house the woman's apparel, the man the man's. But why don't you bring the mantle home again?

MENAECHMUS of Epidamnus. I'll have it brought back.

THE WIFE OF MENAECHMUS of Epidamnus. For your own interest you'll do so, as I think; for you shall never enter the house to-day unless you bring the mantle with you. I'm going home.

PENICULUS. (*to the* WIFE). What's there to be for me, who have given you this assistance?

THE WIFE OF MENAECHMUS of Epidamnus. Your assistance shall be repaid, when anything shall be purloined from your house. (*The* WIFE *goes into the house*.)

PENICULUS. Then, by my troth, that really will never be; for nothing have I at home to lose. May the Gods confound you, both husband and wife. I'll make haste to the Forum, for I see clearly that I've quite fallen out with this family. (*Exit*.)

MENAECHMUS of Epidamnus. My wife thinks that she does me an injury when she shuts me out of doors; as though I hadn't another better place to be admitted into. If I displease you, I must endure it; I shall please Erotium here, who won't be shutting me out of her house, but will be shutting me up in her house rather. Now I'll go; I'll beg her to give me back the mantle that I gave her a while since. I'll purchase another for her—a better one. Hallo! is any one the porter here? (*Knocks at* EROTIUM'S *door.*) Open here, and some one of you call Erotium before the door.

58

Enter EROTIUM, *from her house.*

EROTIUM. Who's enquiring for me here?

MENAECHMUS of Epidamnus. One that's more of an enemy to his own self than to yourself. [8]

EROTIUM. My dear Menaechmus? Why are you standing before the house? Do follow me in-doors.

MENAECHMUS of Epidamnus. Stop. Do you know why it is that I'm come to you?

EROTIUM. I know well; that you may amuse yourself with me.

MENAECHMUS of Epidamnus. Why no, troth, that mantle which I gave you a while since, give it me back, I entreat you; my wife has become acquainted with all the transaction, in its order, just as it happened. I'll procure for you a mantle of twofold greater value than you shall wish.

EROTIUM. Why, I gave it your own self a little while since, that you might take it to the embroiderer's, and that bracelet, too, that you might take it to the goldsmith's that it might be made anew.

MENAECHMUS of Epidamnus. You, gave me the mantle and the bracelet? You'll find 'twas never done. For, indeed, after I gave it you a while ago, and went away to the Forum, I'm but just returning, and now see you for the first time since.

EROTIUM. I see what plan you are upon; that you may defraud me of what I entrusted to you, at that thing you are aiming——

MENAECHMUS of Epidamnus. On my word, I do not ask it for the sake of defrauding you. But I tell you that my wife has discovered the matter.

EROTIUM. Nor did I of my own accord beg you to give it me; of your own accord you yourself brought it me. You gave it me as a present; now you're asking for the same thing back again. I'll put up with it; keep it to yourself; take it away; make use of it, either yourself or your wife, or squeeze it into your money-box [9] even. After this day, that you mayn't be deceived, you shan't set your foot in this house, since you hold me in contempt, who deserve so well of you. Unless you bring money, you'll be disappointed; you can't cajole me. Find some other woman, henceforth, for you to be disappointing.

MENAECHMUS of Epidamnus. By my troth, very angry at last. Hallo! you; stay, I bid you. Come you back. Will you stay now? Will you even for my sake come back? (EROTIUM *goes into her house, and shuts the door*.) She has gone indoors, and shut the house. Now I'm regularly barred out; I have neither any credit at home now, nor with my mistress. I'll go and consult my friends on this matter, as to what they think should be done. (*Exit.*)

FOOTNOTES TO ACT IV.

[1] To remain in wedlock: As already observed in the Notes to the Stichus and the Miles Gloriosus, the facilities for divorce, by reason of incompatibility and other circumstances, were very great among the Romans.

[2] Most worthy and great: "Optumi maximi." This was properly an epithet of Jupiter, and is, perhaps, satirically applied to the "little Gods," the great men of Rome. In the previous line he uses "morus," the Greek word *môros*, signifying "foolish," on account of its resemblance to the word "mores," "manner" or "custom."

[3] Before the people: It is thought that he here refers to the three modes of trial in civil cases among the Romans—"apud populum," before the people in the Comitia centuriata, or full assembly; "in jure," before the "Praetor," or his delegates, the "Recuperatores" or "Judices selecti," "commissioned judges;" and before the Aedile, or city officer. He says, that on being summoned to the "concio," a "cliens" or dependant suddenly accosted him, and insisted on his defending him, which greatly detained him, but that in spite of the worthlessness of his client's cause, he was at last successful in effecting a compromise.

[4] That surety for him: He probably means that he gained time for his client to pay the debt, on condition of his giving bail or security that be would do so within a certain time.

[5] The mantle makes: "Palla pallorem incutit." In his alarm he cannot avoid a pun on the resemblance between "palla," the "mantle," and "pallor," paleness. The meaning is, literally, "the mantle strikes paleness into me;" but an attempt is made in the Translation to imitate the play upon the words.

[6] Such is the return: "Sic datur." Literally, "thus it is given," or "on these terms it is lent." Some Commentators will have it, that these words are accompanied with a slap on the face, in which case they will be equivalent to "there, take that." They may, however, simply mean, "such are the terms" on which you had my mantle, "such are the results of your lending;" her abuse and indignation,

accompanied, perhaps, with a threat, being the "foenus," or "interest" for the loan.

[7] Wish for an owl: "Tu, tu." He alludes to the note of the owl which to the Romans would seem to say "tu, tu" "you, you."

[8] Than to yourself: "Aetati tuae." Literally, "to your age," a circumlocution for "yourself."

[9] Into your money-box: "As you make so much fuss about and it is so valuable, squeeze it up into your money-box."

ACT V.

SCENE I.

Enter MENAECHMUS SOSICLES, *with the mantle on.*

MENAECHMUS SOSICLES. I did very foolishly a while since, in entrusting my purse to Messenio with the money. I suspect he has got himself into some bad house [1] or other.

Enter the WIFE *of Menaechmus of Epidamnus, from the house.*

THE WIFE OF MENAECHMUS of Epidamnus. I'll look out to see how soon my husband is going to return home. But here he is; I see him; I'm all right, he's bringing back the mantle.

MENAECHMUS SOSICLES. (*to himself*). I wonder where Messenio can be walking now.

THE WIFE OF MENAECHMUS of Epidamnus. I'll go and receive the fellow with such language as he deserves. (Accosting him.) Are you not ashamed to come forward in my presence, you disgraceful man, in that garb?

MENAECHMUS SOSICLES. What's the matter? What thing is troubling you, woman?

THE WIFE OF MENAECHMUS of Epidamnus. Do you dare, you shameless fellow, to utter even a single word, or to speak to me?

MENAECHMUS SOSICLES. Pray, what wrong have I committed, that I shouldn't dare to speak to you?

THE WIFE OF MENAECHMUS of Epidamnus. Do you ask me? O dear, the impudent audacity of the fellow!

MENAECHMUS SOSICLES. Don't you know, madam, for what reason the Greeks used to say that Hecuba was a bitch? [2]

THE WIFE OF MENAECHMUS of Epidamnus. I don't know, indeed.

MENAECHMUS SOSICLES. Because Hecuba used to do the same thing that you are now doing. She used to heap all kinds of imprecations on every one she saw; and, therefore, for that reason she was properly begun to be called a bitch.

THE WIFE OF MENAECHMUS of Epidamnus. I can't put up with this disgraceful conduct of yours; for I had rather see my life that of a widow, than endure this vile conduct of yours that you are guilty of.

MENAECHMUS SOSICLES. What is it to me, whether you are able to endure to live in the married state, or whether you will separate from your husband? Is it thus the fashion here to tell these stories to a stranger on his arrival?

THE WIFE OF MENAECHMUS of Epidamnus. What stories? I say, I'll not endure it henceforth, but live separate rather than put up with these ways.

MENAECHMUS SOSICLES. Troth, so far indeed as I'm concerned, do live separate, even so long as Jupiter shall hold his sway.

THE WIFE OF MENAECHMUS of Epidamnus. By heavens, I'll certainly now send for my father, and I'll tell him your disgraceful conduct that you are guilty of. Go, Decio (*calling to a* SERVANT), seek for my father, that he may come along with you to me; tell him that occasion has arisen for it. I'll. now disclose to him this disgraceful conduct of yours.

MENAECHMUS SOSICLES. Are you in your senses? What disgraceful conduct of mine?

THE WIFE OF MENAECHMUS of Epidamnus. When you filch from home my mantle and gold trinkets, without the knowledge of your wife, and carry them off to your mistress. Don't I state this correctly?

MENAECHMUS SOSICLES. O dear! madam, by my faith, you are both very bold and very perverse. Do you dare to say (pointing at the mantle) that this was stolen from you which another woman gave me, for me to get it trimmed?

THE WIFE OF MENAECHMUS of Epidamnus. A little while since you didn't deny that you had purloined it from me; do you now hold up that same before my eyes? Are you not ashamed?

MENAECHMUS SOSICLES. By my faith, madam, I entreat you, if you know, show me what I'm to drink [3], by means of which I may put up with your impertinence. What person you are taking me to be, I don't know; I know you just as well as Parthaon. [4]

THE WIFE OF MENAECHMUS of Epidamnus. If you laugh at me, still, i' troth, you can't do so at him; my father, I mean, who's coming here. Why don't you look back? Do you know that person?

MENAECHMUS SOSICLES. Just as well as Calchas [5] do I know him; I have seen him on that same day on which I have seen yourself before this present day.

THE WIFE OF MENAECHMUS of Epidamnus. Do you deny that you know me? Do you deny that you know my father?

MENAECHMUS SOSICLES. Troth, I shall say the same thing, if you choose to bring your grandfather.

THE WIFE OF MENAECHMUS of Epidamnus. I' faith, you do this and other things just in a like fashion.

SCENE II.

Enter an OLD MAN, *hobbling with a stick.*

OLD MAN According as my age permits, and as there is occasion to do so, I'll push on my steps and make haste to get along. But how far from easy 'tis for me, I'm not mistaken as to that. For my agility forsakes me, and I am beset with age; I carry my body weighed down; my strength has deserted me. How grievous a pack upon one's back is age. For when it comes, it brings very many and very grievous particulars, were I now to recount all of which, my speech would be too long. But this matter is a trouble to my mind and heart, what this business can possibly be on account of which my daughter suddenly requires me to come to her, and doesn't first let me know what's the matter, what she wants, or why she sends for me. But pretty nearly do I know now what's the matter; I suspect that some quarrel has arisen with her husband. So are these women wont to do, who, presuming on their portions, and haughty, require their husbands to be obedient to them; and they as well full oft are not without fault. But still there are bounds, within which a wife ought to be put up with. By my troth, my daughter never sends for her father to come to her except when either something has been done wrong, or there is a cause for quarrelling. But whatever it is, I shall now know. And see, I perceive her herself before the house, and her husband in a pensive mood. 'Tis the same as I suspected. I'll accost her.

THE WIFE OF MENAECHMUS of Epidamnus. I'll go and meet him. May every happiness attend you, my father.

OLD MAN. Happiness attend you. Do I find you in good spirits? Do you bid me be fetched in happy mood? Why are you sorrowful? And why does he (*pointing at* MENAECHMUS) in anger stand apart from you? Something, I know not what, are you two wrangling about [6] between you. Say, in few words, which of the two is in fault: no long speeches, though.

THE WIFE OF MENAECHMUS of Epidamnus. For my part, I've done nothing wrong; as to that point do I at once make you easy, father. But I cannot live or remain here on any account; you must take me away hence immediately.

OLD MAN. Why, what's the matter?

THE WIFE OF MENAECHMUS of Epidamnus. I am made a laughing-stock of, father.

OLD MAN. By whom?

THE WIFE OF MENAECHMUS of Epidamnus. By him to whom you gave me, my husband.

OLD MAN. Look at that — a quarrel now. How often, I wonder, have I told you to be cautious, that neither should be coming to me with your complaints.

THE WIFE OF MENAECHMUS of Epidamnus. How, my father, can I possibly guard against that?

OLD MAN. Do you ask me? * * * * * unless you don't wish. How often have I told you to be compliant to your husband. Don't be watching what he does, where he goes, or what matter he's about.

THE WIFE OF MENAECHMUS of Epidamnus. Why, but he's in love with a courtesan here close by.

OLD MAN. He is exceedingly wise: and for this painstaking of yours, I would even have him love her the more.

THE WIFE OF MENAECHMUS of Epidamnus. He drinks there, too.

OLD MAN. And will he really drink the less for you, whether it shall please him to do so there or anywhere else? Plague on it, what assurance is this? On the same principle, you would wish to hinder him from engaging to dine out, or from receiving any other person at his own house. Do you want husbands to be your servants? You might as well expect, on the same principle, to be giving him out his task, and bidding him sit among the female servants and card wool.

THE WIFE OF MENAECHMUS of Epidamnus. Why, surely, father, I've sent for you not to be my advocate, but my husband's: on this side you stand [7], on the other you plead the cause.

OLD MAN. If he has done wrong in anything, so much the more shall I censure him than I've censured you. Since he keeps you provided for and well clothed, and finds you amply in female servants and provisions, 'tis better, madam, to entertain kindly feelings.

THE WIFE OF MENAECHMUS of Epidamnus. But he purloins from me gold trinkets and mantles from out of the chests at home; he plunders me, and secretly carries off my ornaments to harlots.

OLD MAN. He does wrong, if he does that; if he does not do it, you do wrong in accusing him when innocent.

THE WIFE OF MENAECHMUS of Epidamnus. Why at this moment, even, he has got a mantle, father, and a bracelet, which he had carried off to her; now, because I came to know of it, he brings them back.

OLD MAN. I'll know from himself, then, how it happened. I'll go up to this man and accost him. (*Goes up to* MENAECHMUS.) Tell me this, Menaechmus, what you two are disputing about, that I may know. Why are you pensive? And why does she in anger stand apart from you?

MENAECHMUS SOSICLES. Whoever you are, whatever is your name, old gentleman, I call to witness supreme Jove and the Deities——

OLD MAN. For what reason, or what matter of all matters?

MENAECHMUS SOSICLES. That I have neither done wrong to that woman, who is accusing me of having purloined this (pointing to the mantle) away from her at home * * * * * and which she solemnly swears that I did take away. If ever I set foot inside of her house where she lives, I wish that I may become the most wretched of all wretched men.

OLD MAN. Are you in your senses to wish this, or to deny that you ever set foot in that house where you live, you downright madman?

MENAECHMUS SOSICLES. Do you say, old gentleman, that I live in this house? (*Pointing at the house.*)

OLD MAN. Do you deny it?

MENAECHMUS SOSICLES. By my faith, certainly do deny it.

OLD MAN. In your fun you are going too far in denying it; unless you flitted elsewhere this last night. Step this way, please, daughter. (*To the* WIFE.) What do you say? Have you removed from this house?

THE WIFE OF MENAECHMUS of Epidamnus. To what place, or for what reason, prithee?

OLD MAN. I' faith, I don't know.

THE WIFE OF MENAECHMUS of Epidamnus. He's surely making fun of you.

OLD MAN. Can't you keep yourself quiet? Now, Menaechmus, you really have joked long enough; now do seriously attend to this matter.

MENAECHMUS SOSICLES. Prithee, what have I to do with you? Whence or what person are you? Is your mind right, or hers, in fact, who is an annoyance to me in every way?

THE WIFE OF MENAECHMUS of Epidamnus. Don't you see how his eyes sparkle? How a green colour [8] is arising on his temples and his forehead; look how his eyes do glisten * * * * *

MENAECHMUS SOSICLES. O me! They say I'm mad, whereas they of themselves are mad.

THE WIFE OF MENAECHMUS of Epidamnus. How he yawns, as he stretches himself. What am I to do now, my father?

OLD MAN. Step this way, my daughter, as far as ever you can from him.

MENAECHMUS SOSICLES. (*aside*). What is there better for me than, since they say I'm mad, to pretend that I am mad, that I may frighten them away from me? (*He dances about.*) Evoë, Bacchus, ho! Bromius [9], in what forest dost thou invite me to the chase? I hear thee, but I cannot get away from this spot, so much does this raving mad female cur watch me on the left side. And behind there is that other old he-goat, who many a time in his life has proved the destruction of an innocent fellow-citizen by his false testimony.

OLD MAN. (*shaking his stick at him*). Woe to your head.

MENAECHMUS SOSICLES. Lo! by his oracle, Apollo bids me burn out her eyes with blazing torches. (*He points with his fingers at her.*)

THE WIFE OF MENAECHMUS of Epidamnus. I'm undone, my father; he's threatening to burn my eyes out.

OLD MAN. Hark you, daughter.

THE WIFE OF MENAECHMUS of Epidamnus. What's the matter? What are we to do?

OLD MAN. What if I call the servants out here? I'll go bring some to take him away hence, and bind him at home, before he makes any further disturbance.

MENAECHMUS SOSICLES. (*aside*). So now; I think now if I don't adopt some plan for myself, these people will be carrying me off home to their house. (Aloud.) Dost thou forbid me to spare my fists at all upon her face, unless she does at once get out of my sight to utter and extreme perdition? I will do what thou dost bid me, Apollo. (*Runs after her.*)

OLD MAN. (*to the* WIFE). Away with you home as soon as possible, lest he should knock you down.

THE WIFE OF MENAECHMUS of Epidamnus. I'm off. Watch him, my father, I entreat you, that he mayn't go anywhere hence. Am I not a wretched woman to hear these things? (*She goes into her house.*)

MENAECHMUS SOSICLES. (*aside*). I've got rid of her not so badly. (*Aloud*). Now as for this most filthy, long-bearded, palsied Tithonus, who is said to have had Cygnus for his father [10], you bid me break in pieces his limbs, and bones, and members with that walking-stick which he himself is holding.

OLD MAN. Punishment shall be inflicted if you touch me indeed, or if you come nearer to me.

MENAECHMUS SOSICLES. (*shouting aloud*). I will do what thou dost bid me; I will take a two-edged axe, and I will hew this old fellow to his very bones, and I will chop his entrails into mincemeat.

OLD MAN. (*retreating as far as he can*). Why really against that must I take care and precaution. As he threatens, I'm quite in dread of him, lest he should do me some mischief.

MENAECHMUS SOSICLES. (*jumping and raising his arms*). Many things dost thou bid me do, Apollo. Now thou dost order me to take the yoked horses, unbroke and fierce, and to mount the chariot, that I may crush to pieces this aged, stinking, toothless lion. Now have I mounted the chariot; now do I hold the reins; now is the whip in my hand. Speed onward, ye steeds, let the sound of your hoofs be heard; in your swift course let the rapid pace of your feet [11] be redoubled. (*Points at the* OLD MAN *as he pretends to gallop.*)

OLD MAN. Are you threatening me with your yoked steeds?

MENAECHMUS SOSICLES. Lo! again, Apollo, thou dost bid me to make an onset against him who is standing here, and to murder him. But what person is this that is tearing me hence by the hair down from the chariot? He revokes thy commands and the decree of Apollo.

OLD MAN. Alas! a severe and obstinate malady, i' faith. By our trust in you, ye Gods * * * * * even this person who is now mad, how well he was a little time since. All on a sudden has so great a distemper attacked him. I'll go now and fetch a physician as fast as I can. (*Exit.*)

MENAECHMUS SOSICLES. Prithee, are these persons gone now out of my sight, who are compelling me by force, while in my wits, to be mad? Why do I delay to be off to the ship, while I can in safety?

* * * * * And all of you (*to the* SPECTATORS), if the old gentleman should return, I beg not to tell him, now, by what street I fled away hence. (*Exit.*)

SCENE III.

Enter the OLD MAN, *very slowly.*

OLD MAN. My bones ache with sitting, my eyes with watching, while waiting for the Doctor, till he returned from his business. At last the troublesome fellow has with difficulty got away from his patients. He says that he has set a broken leg for Aesculapius [12], and an arm for Apollo. I'm now thinking whether I'm to say that I'm bringing a doctor or a carpenter [13]. But, see, here he comes.—Do get on with your ant's pace.

SCENE IV.

Enter a DOCTOR.

DOCTOR. What did you say was his disorder? Tell me, respected sir. Is he harassed by sprites [14], or is he frenzied? Let me know. Is it lethargy, or is it dropsy, that possesses him?

OLD MAN. Why, I'm bringing you for that reason, that you may tell me that, and make him convalescent.

DOCTOR. That indeed is a very easy matter. Why, I shall heal innumerable times as many [15] in the day.

OLD MAN. I wish him to be treated with great attention.

DOCTOR. That he shall be healed, I promise that on my word; so with great attention will I treat him for you.

OLD MAN. Why, see! here's the man himself.

DOCTOR. Let's watch what matter he's about. (*They stand aside.*)

SCENE V.

Enter MENAECHMUS *of Epidamnus.*

MENAECHMUS of Epidamnus. (to himself) . By my faith, this day has certainly fallen out perverse and adverse for me, since the Parasite, who has filled me full of disgrace and terror, has made that all known, which I supposed I was doing secretly; my own Ulysses [16], who has brought so great evil on his king—a fellow that, by my troth, if I only live, I'll soon finish his life [17]. But I'm a fool, who call that his, which is my own. With my own victuals and at my own expense has he been supported; of existence will I deprive the fellow. But the Courtesan has done this in a way worthy of her, just as the harlot's habit is: because I ask for the mantle, that it may be returned again to my wife, she declares that she has given it me. O dear! By my faith, I do live a wretched man.

OLD MAN. (*apart*). Do you hear what he says?

DOCTOR. (*apart*). He declares that he is wretched.

OLD MAN. (*apart*). I wish you to accost him.

DOCTOR. (*going up to him*). Save you, Menaechmus. Prithee, why do you bare your arm? Don't you know how much mischief you are now doing to that disease of yours?

MENAECHMUS of Epidamnus. Why don't you go hang yourself?

OLD MAN. What think you now?

DOCTOR. What shouldn't I think? This case can't be treated with even ointment of hellebore. But what have you to say, Menaechmus?

MENAECHMUS of Epidamnus. What do you want?

DOCTOR. Tell me this that I ask of you; do you drink white wine or dark-coloured?

MENAECHMUS of Epidamnus. What need have you to enquire?

DOCTOR. * * * * *

MENAECHMUS of Epidamnus. Why don't you go to utter perdition?

OLD MAN. Troth, he's now beginning to be attacked with the fit.

MENAECHMUS of Epidamnus. Why don't you ask whether I'm wont to eat dark bread, or purple, or yellow? Or whether I'm wont to eat birds with scales, or fish with wings?

OLD MAN. Dear, dear! (*To the* DOCTOR.) Don't you hear how deliriously he talks? Why do you delay to give him something by way of a potion, before his raving overtakes him?

DOCTOR. Stop a little; I'll question him on some other matters as well.

OLD MAN. You are killing me [18] by your prating.

DOCTOR. (to MENAECHMUS) . Tell me this; are your eyes ever in the habit of becoming hard? [19]

MENAECHMUS of Epidamnus. What? Do you take me to be a locust [20], you most worthless fellow?

DOCTOR. Tell me, now, do your bowels ever rumble that you know of?

MENAECHMUS of Epidamnus. When I'm full, they don't rumble at all; when I'm hungry, then they do rumble.

DOCTOR. I' faith, he really gave me that answer not like an insane person. Do you always sleep soundly until daylight? Do you easily go to sleep when in bed?

MENAECHMUS of Epidamnus. I sleep throughout if * * * * * I go to sleep if I have paid my money to him to whom I owe it.

DOCTOR. * * * * *

MENAECHMUS of Epidamnus. (to the DOCTOR) . May Jupiter and all the Divinities confound you, you questioner.

DOCTOR. (*aside*) . Now this person begins to rave. (*To the* OLD MAN.) From those expressions do you take care of yourself.

OLD MAN. Why, he's now really quite favourable in his language, in comparison with what he was a short time since; for, a little while ago, he was saying that his wife was a raving cur.

MENAECHMUS of Epidamnus. What did I say?

OLD MAN. You were raving, I say.

MENAECHMUS of Epidamnus. What, I?

OLD MAN. You there; who threatened as well to ride me down with your yoked steeds.

MENAECHMUS of Epidamnus. * * * * *

OLD MAN. I myself saw you do this; I myself accuse you of this.

MENAECHMUS of Epidamnus. And I know that you stole [21] the sacred crown of Jupiter; and that on that account you were confined in prison; and after you were let out, I know that you were beaten with rods in the bilboes; I know, too, that you murdered your father and sold your mother. Don't I give this abuse in answer for your abuse, like a sane person?

OLD MAN. I' faith, Doctor, whatever you are about to do, prithee, do it quickly. Don't you see that the man is raving?

DOCTOR. Do you know what's the best for you to do? Have him taken to my house.

OLD MAN. Do you think so?

DOCTOR. Why should I not? There at my own discretion I shall be able to treat the man.

OLD MAN. Do just as you please.

DOCTOR. (*to* MENAECHMUS) . I'll make you drink hellebore some twenty days.

MENAECHMUS of Epidamnus. But, hanging up [22], I'll flog you with a whip for thirty days.

DOCTOR. (*to the* OLD MAN) . Go fetch some men to take him off to my house.

OLD MAN. How many are sufficient?

DOCTOR. Since I see him thus raving, four, no less.

OLD MAN. They shall be here this instant. Do you keep an eye on him, Doctor.

DOCTOR. Why, no, I shall go home that the things may be got ready, which are necessary to be prepared. Bid your servants carry him to my house.

OLD MAN. I'll make him be there just now.

DOCTOR. I'm off.

OLD MAN. Farewell. (*Exeunt* OLD MAN *and* DOCTOR, *separately.*)

MENAECHMUS of Epidamnus. My father-in-law is gone, the Doctor is gone; I'm alone. O Jupiter! Why is it that these people say I'm mad? Why, in fact, since I was born, I have never for a single day been ill. I'm neither mad, nor do I commence strifes or quarrels. In health myself, I see others well; I know people, I address them. Is it that they who falsely say I'm mad, are mad themselves? What shall I do now? I wish to go home; but my wife doesn't allow me; and here (*pointing to* EROTIUM'S *house*) no one admits me. Most unfortunately has this fallen out. Here will I still remain; at night, at least, I shall be let into the house, I trust. (*Stands near his door.*)

SCENE VI.

Enter MESSENIO.

MESSENIO. (*to himself*). This is the proof of a good servant, who takes care of his master's business, looks after it, arranges it, thinks about it, in the absence of his master diligently to attend to the affairs of his master, as much so as if he himself were present, or even better. It is proper that his back [23] should be of more consequence than his appetite, his legs than his stomach, whose heart is rightly placed. Let him bear in mind, those who are good for nothing, what reward is given them by their masters—lazy, worthless fellows. Stripes, fetters, the mill, weariness, hunger, sharp cold; these are the rewards of idleness. This evil do I terribly stand in awe of. Wherefore 'tis sure that to be good is better than to be bad. Much more readily do I submit to words, stripes I do detest; and I eat what is ground much more readily than supply it ground by myself [24]. Therefore do I obey the command of my master, carefully and diligently do I observe it; and in such manner do I pay obedience, as I think is for the interest of my back. And that course does profit me. Let others be just as they take it to be their interest; I shall be just as I ought to be. If I adhere to that, I shall avoid faultiness; so that I am in readiness for my master on all occasions, I shall not be much afraid. The time is near, when, for these deeds of mine, my master will give his reward. After I had deposited the goods and the servants in the inn, as he ordered me, thus am I come to meet him. (*Going to the door of* EROTIUM'S *house.*) Now I'll knock at the door, that he may know that I'm here, and that out of this thick wood [25] of peril I may get my master safe out of doors. But I'm afraid that I'm come too late, after the battle has been fought.

SCENE VII.

Enter the OLD MAN, *with* SERVANTS.

OLD MAN. (*to the* SERVANTS). By Gods and men, I tell you prudently to pay regard to my commands, as to what I have commanded and do command. Take care that this person is carried at once upon your shoulders to the surgery, unless, indeed, you set no value upon your legs or your sides. Take care each of you to regard at a straw whatever threats he shall utter. What are you standing for? Why are you hesitating? By this you ought to have had him carried off on your shoulders. I'll go to the Doctor; I'll be there ready when you shall come.

Exit. The SERVANTS *gather around* MENAECHMUS.

MENAECHMUS of Epidamnus. I'm undone. What business is this? Why are these men running towards me, pray? What do you want? What do you seek? Why do you stand around me? (*They seize and drag him.*) Whither are you dragging me? Whither are you carrying me? I'm undone. I entreat your assistance, citizens, men of Epidamnus, come and help me. (*To the men.*) Why don't you let me go?

MESSENIO. (*running towards them*). O ye immortal Gods, I beseech you, what do I behold with my eyes? Some fellows, I know not who, are most disgracefully carrying off my master upon their shoulders.

MENAECHMUS of Epidamnus. Who is it that ventures to bring me aid?

MESSENIO. I, master, and right boldly. (*Aloud.*) O shameful and scandalous deed, citizens of Epidamnus, for my master, here in a town enjoying peace, to be carried off, in daylight, in the street, who came to you a free man. Let him go.

MENAECHMUS of Epidamnus. Prithee, whoever you are, do lend me your aid, and don't suffer so great an outrage to be signally committed against me.

MESSENIO. Aye, I'll give you my aid, and I'll defend you, and zealously succour you. I'll never let you come to harm; 'tis fitter that I myself should come to harm. I'll now make a sowing on the faces of these fellows, and there I'll plant my fists. I' faith, you're carrying this person off this day at your own extreme hazard. Let him go. (*He lays about him.*)

MENAECHMUS of Epidamnus. (*fighting with them*). I've got hold of this fellow's eye.

MESSENIO. Make the socket of his eye be seen in his head. You rascals! you villains! you robbers!

THE SERVANTS (*severally*). We are undone. Troth, now, prithee, do——

MESSENIO. Let him go then.

MENAECHMUS of Epidamnus. What business have you to touch me? Thump them with your fists.

MESSENIO. Come, begone, fly hence to utter perdition with you. (*Three run away.*) Here's for you, too (*giving the fourth one a punch*); because you are the last to yield, you shall have this for a reward. (*They all disappear.*) Right well have I marked his face, and quite to my liking. Troth, now, master, I really did come to your help just now in the nick of time.

MENAECHMUS of Epidamnus. And may the Gods, young man, whoever you are, ever bless you. For, had it not been for you, I should never have survived this day until sunset.

MESSENIO. By my troth, then, master, if you do right, you will give me my freedom.

MENAECHMUS of Epidamnus. I, give you your freedom?

MESSENIO. Doubtless: since, master, I have saved you.

MENAECHMUS of Epidamnus. How's this? Young man, you are mistaken.

MESSENIO. How, mistaken?

MENAECHMUS of Epidamnus. By father Jove, I solemnly swear that I am not your master.

MESSENIO. Will you not hold your peace?

MENAECHMUS of Epidamnus. I'm telling no lie; nor did any servant of mine ever do such a thing as you have done for me.

MESSENIO. In that case, then, let me go free, if you deny that I am your servant.

MENAECHMUS of Epidamnus. By my faith, so far, indeed, as I'm concerned, be free, and go where you like.

MESSENIO. That is, you order me to do so?

MENAECHMUS of Epidamnus. I' faith, I do order you, if I have aught of authority over you.

MESSENIO. Save you, my patron. Since you seriously give me my freedom, I rejoice.

MENAECHMUS of Epidamnus. I' faith, I really do believe you.

MESSENIO. But, my patron, I do entreat you that you won't command me any the less now than when I was your servant. With you will I dwell, and when you go I'll go home together with you. Wait for me here; I'll now go to the inn, and bring back the luggage and the money for you. The purse, with the money for our journey, is fast sealed up in the wallet; I'll bring it just now here to you.

MENAECHMUS of Epidamnus. Bring it carefully.

MESSENIO. I'll give it back safe to you just as you gave it to me. Do you wait for me here. (*Exit MESSENIO.*)

MENAECHMUS of Epidamnus. Very wonderful things have really happened this day to me in wonderful ways. Some deny that I am he who I am, and shut me out of doors; others say that I am he who I am not, and will have it that they are my servants. He for instance, who said that he was going for the money, to whom I gave his freedom just now. Since he says that he will bring me a purse with money, if he does bring it [26], I'll say that he may go free from me where he pleases, lest at a time when he shall have come to his senses he should ask the money of me. My father-in-law and the Doctor were saying that I am mad. Whatever it is, it is a wonderful affair. These things appear to me not at all otherwise than dreams. Now I'll go in the house to this Courtesan, although she is angry with me; if I can prevail upon her to restore the mantle for me to take back home. (*He goes into* EROTIUM'S *house*.)

SCENE VIII.

Enter MENAECHMUS SOSICLES *and* MESSENIO.

MENAECHMUS SOSICLES. Do you dare affirm, audacious fellow, that I have ever met you this day since the time when I ordered you to come here to meet me?

MESSENIO. Why, I just now rescued you before this house, when four men were carrying you off upon their shoulders. You invoked the aid of all Gods and men, when I ran up and delivered you by main force, fighting, and in spite of them. For this reason, because I rescued you, you set me at liberty. When I said that I was going for the money and the luggage, you ran before to meet me as quickly as you could, in order that you might deny what you did.

MENAECHMUS SOSICLES. I, bade you go away a free man?

MESSENIO. Certainly.

MENAECHMUS SOSICLES. Why, on the contrary, 'tis most certain that I myself would rather become a slave than ever give you your freedom.

SCENE IX.

Enter MENAECHMUS *of Epidamnus, from* EROTIUM'S *house.*

MENAECHMUS of Epidamnus. (*at the door, to* EROTIUM *within*) . If you are ready to swear by your eyes, by my troth, not a bit the more for that reason, most vile woman, will you make it that I took away the mantle and the bracelet to-day.

MESSENIO. Immortal Gods, what do I see?

MENAECHMUS SOSICLES. What do you see?

MESSENIO. Your resemblance in a mirror.

MENAECHMUS SOSICLES. What's the matter?

MESSENIO. 'Tis your image; 'tis as like as possible.

MENAECHMUS SOSICLES. (*catching sight of the other*). Troth, it really is not unlike, so far as I know my own form.

MENAECHMUS of Epidamnus. (*to* MESSENIO) . O young man, save you, you who preserved me, whoever you are.

MESSENIO. By my troth, young man, prithee, tell me your name, unless it's disagreeable.

MENAECHMUS of Epidamnus. I' faith, you've not so deserved of me, that it should be disagreeable for me to tell what you wish. My name is Menaechmus.

MENAECHMUS SOSICLES. Why, by my troth, so is mine.

MENAECHMUS of Epidamnus. I am a Sicilian, of Syracuse.

MENAECHMUS SOSICLES. Troth, the same is my native country.

MENAECHMUS of Epidamnus. What is it that I hear of you?

MENAECHMUS SOSICLES. That which is the fact.

MESSENIO. (*To* MENAECHMUS SOSICLES, *by mistake*). I know this person myself (*pointing to the other* MENAECHMUS); he is my master, I really am his servant; but I did think I belonged to this other. (*To* MENAECHMUS *of Epidamnus, by mistake*.) I took him to be you; to him, too, did I give some trouble. (*To his master*.) Pray, pardon me if I have said aught foolishly or unadvisedly to you.

MENAECHMUS SOSICLES. You seem to me to be mad. Don't you remember that together with me you disembarked from board ship to-day?

MESSENIO. Why, really, you say what's right—you are my master; (*to* MENAECHMUS *of Epidamnus*) do you look out for a servant. (*To his master*.) To you my greetings (*to* MENAECHMUS *of Epidamnus*) to you, farewell. This, I say, is Menaechmus.

MENAECHMUS of Epidamnus. But I say I am.

MENAECHMUS SOSICLES. What story's this? Are you Menaechmus?

MENAECHMUS of Epidamnus. I say that I'm the son of Moschus, who was my father.

MENAECHMUS SOSICLES. Are you the son of my father?

MENAECHMUS of Epidamnus. Aye, I really am, young man, of my own father. I don't want to claim your father, nor to take possession of him from you.

MESSENIO. Immortal Gods, what unhoped-for hope do you bestow on me, as I suspect. For unless my mind misleads me, these are the two twin-brothers; for they mention alike their native country and their father. I'll call my master aside—Menaechmus.

BOTH OF THE MENAECHMI. What do you want?

MESSENIO. I don't want you both. But which of you was brought here in the ship with me?

MENAECHMUS of Epidamnus. Not I.

MENAECHMUS SOSICLES. But 'twas I.

MESSENIO. You, then, I want. Step this way. (*They go aside.*)

MENAECHMUS SOSICLES. I've stepped aside now. What's the matter?

MESSENIO. This man is either an impostor, or he is your twin-brother. But I never beheld one person more like another person. Neither water, believe me, is ever more like to water nor milk to milk, than he is to you, and you likewise to him; besides, he speaks of the same native country and father. 'Tis better for us to accost him and make further enquiries of him.

MENAECHMUS SOSICLES. I' faith, but you've given me good advice, and I return you thanks. Troth, now, prithee, do continue to lend me your assistance. If you discover that this is my brother, be you a free man.

MESSENIO. I hope I shall.

MENAECHMUS SOSICLES. I too hope that it will be so.

MESSENIO. (*to* MENAECHMUS *of Epidamnus*) . How say you? I think you said that you are called Menaechmus?

MENAECHMUS of Epidamnus. I did so indeed.

MESSENIO. (*pointing to his master*). His name, too, is Menaechmus. You said that you were born at Syracuse, in Sicily; he was born there. You said that Moschus was your father; he was his as well. Now both of you can be giving help to me and to yourselves at the same time.

MENAECHMUS of Epidamnus. You have deserved that you should beg nothing but what you should obtain that which you desire. Free as I am, I'll serve you as though you. had bought me for money.

MESSENIO. I have a hope that I shall find that you two are twin-born brothers, born of one mother and of one father on the same day.

MENAECHMUS of Epidamnus. You mention wondrous things. I wish that you could effect what you've promised.

MESSENIO. I can. But attend now, both of you, and tell me that which I shall ask.

MENAECHMUS of Epidamnus. Ask as you please, I'll answer you. I'll not conceal anything that I know.

MESSENIO. Isn't your name Menaechmus?

MENAECHMUS of Epidamnus. I own it.

MESSENIO. Isn't it yours as well?

MENAECHMUS SOSICLES. It is.

MESSENIO. Do you say that Moschus was your father?

MENAECHMUS of Epidamnus. Truly, I do say so.

MENAECHMUS SOSICLES. And mine as well.

MESSENIO. Are you of Syracuse?

MENAECHMUS of Epidamnus. Certainly.

MESSENIO. And you?

MENAECHMUS SOSICLES. Why not the same?

MESSENIO. Hitherto the marks agree perfectly well. Still lend me your attention. (*To* MENAECHMUS.) Tell me, what do you remember at the greatest distance of time in your native country?

MENAECHMUS of Epidamnus. When I went with my father to Tarentum to traffic; and afterwards how I strayed away from my father among the people, and was carried away thence.

MENAECHMUS SOSICLES. Supreme Jupiter, preserve me!

MESSENIO. (*to* MENAECHMUS SOSICLES) . Why do you exclaim? Why don't you hold your peace? (*To* MENAECHMUS.) How many years old were you when your father took you from your native country?

MENAECHMUS of Epidamnus. Seven years old; for just then my teeth were changing for the first time. And never since then have I seen my father.

MESSENIO. Well, how many sons of you had your father then?

MENAECHMUS of Epidamnus. As far as I now remember, two.

MESSENIO. Which of the two was the older—you or the other?

MENAECHMUS of Epidamnus. Both were just alike in age.

MESSENIO. How can that be?

MENAECHMUS of Epidamnus. We two were twins.

MENAECHMUS SOSICLES. The Gods wish to bless me.

MESSENIO. (*to* MENAECHMUS SOSICLES). If you interrupt, I shall hold my tongue.

MENAECHMUS SOSICLES. Rather than that, I'll hold my tongue.

MESSENIO. Tell me, were you both of the same name?

MENAECHMUS of Epidamnus. By no means; for my name was what it is now Menaechmus; the other they then used to call Sosicles.

MENAECHMUS SOSICLES. (*embracing his brother*). I recognize the proofs, I cannot refrain from embracing him. My own twin-brother, blessings on you; I am Sosicles.

MENAECHMUS of Epidamnus. How then was the name of Menaechmus afterwards given to you?

MENAECHMUS SOSICLES. After word was brought to us that you * * * * * and that my father was dead, my grandfather changed it; the name that was yours he gave to me.

MENAECHMUS of Epidamnus. I believe that it did so happen as you say. But answer me this.

MENAECHMUS SOSICLES. Ask it of me.

MENAECHMUS of Epidamnus. What was the name of our mother?

MENAECHMUS SOSICLES. Teuximarcha.

MENAECHMUS of Epidamnus. That quite agrees. (*He again embraces him.*) O welcome, unhoped-for brother, whom after many years I now behold.

MENAECHMUS SOSICLES. And you, whom with many and anxious labours I have ever been seeking up to this time, and whom I rejoice at being found.

MESSENIO. (*to his master*). It was for this reason that this Courtesan called you by his name; she thought that you were he, I suppose, when she invited you to breakfast.

MENAECHMUS of Epidamnus. Why, faith, to-day I ordered a breakfast to be got ready here (*pointing to* EROTIUM'S *house*) for me, unknown to my wife; a mantle which a short time since I filched from home, to her I gave it.

MENAECHMUS SOSICLES. Do you say, brother, that this is the mantle which I'm wearing?

MENAECHMUS of Epidamnus. How did this come to you?

MENAECHMUS SOSICLES. The Courtesan who took me here (*pointing to* EROTIUM'S *house*) to breakfast, said that I had given it to her. I breakfasted very pleasantly; I drank and entertained myself with my mistress; she gave me the mantle and this golden trinket. (*Showing the bracelet.*) * * * * *

MENAECHMUS of Epidamnus. I' faith, I'm glad if any luck has befallen you on my account; for when she invited you to her house, she supposed it to be me.

MESSENIO. Do you make any objection that I should be free as you commanded?

MENAECHMUS of Epidamnus. He asks, brother, what's very fair and very just Do it for my sake.

MENAECHMUS SOSICLES. (*touching* MESSENIO'S *shoulder*) . Be thou a free man.

MENAECHMUS of Epidamnus. I am glad, Messenio, that you are free.

MESSENIO. Why, better auspices [27] were required that I should be free for life. * * * * *

MENAECHMUS SOSICLES. Since these matters, brother, have turned out to our wishes, let us both return to our native land.

MENAECHMUS of Epidamnus. Brother, I'll do as you wish. I'll have an auction here, and sell whatever I have. In the meantime, brother, let's now go in-doors.

MENAECHMUS SOSICLES. Be it so.

MESSENIO. Do you know what I ask of you?

MENAECHMUS of Epidamnus. What?

MESSENIO. To give me the place of auctioneer.

MENAECHMUS of Epidamnus. It shall be given you.

MESSENIO. Would you like the auction, then, to be proclaimed at once? For what day?

MENAECHMUS of Epidamnus. On the seventh day hence.

MESSENIO. (*coming forward, and speaking in a loud voice*). An auction of the property of Menaechmus will certainly take place on the morning of the seventh day hence. His slaves, furniture, house, and farms, will be sold. All will go for whatever they'll fetch at ready money prices. His wife, too, will be sold as well, if any purchaser shall come. I think that by the entire sale Menaechmus will hardly get fifty hundred thousand [28] sesterces. (*To the* SPECTATORS.) Now, Spectators, fare you well, and give us loud applause. [29]

FOOTNOTES TO ACT V.

[1] Into some bad house: The "ganeae" or "ganea" were, probably, very similar to the "popinae," the loose character of which, and the "thermopolia," has been alluded to in a preceding Note.

[2] Hecuba was a bitch: Hecuba was the daughter of Cisseus or of Dymas, and the wife of Priam, King of Troy. In the distribution of the spoil, after the siege of Troy, she fell to the share of Ulysses, and became his slave, but lied soon after in Thrace. Servius alleges, with Plautus, that the Greeks circulated the story of her transformation into a bitch, because she was perpetually railing at them to provoke them to put her to death, rather than condemn her to the life of a slave. According to Strabo and Pomponius Mela, in their time the place of her burial was still to be seen in Thrace. It was called *kunos sêma*, "the Tomb of the bitch." Euripides, in his "Hecuba," has not followed this tradition, but represents her as complaining that the Greeks had chained her to the door of Agamemnon like a dog.

[3] What I'm to drink: Some Commentators think that he is asking for a medical potion, to help him to swallow down the "petulantia," or insulting conduct. This supposition does not seem necessary, for even a draught of water would have the same effect in such a case.

[4] As well as Parthaon: Parthaon was the father of Oeneus, King of Aetolia, the father of Deianeira, the wife of Hercules. The name is used to signify a person who lived so long ago that it was impossible to know him.

[5] As well as Calchas: Calchas, the son of Thestor, was a famous soothsayer, who accompanied the Grecian army in the expedition against Troy.

[6] Wrangling about: "Velitati estis," literally, "have been skirmishing." The figure is derived from the "velites," the light-armed soldiers of the Roman army, who were not drawn up in rank and file, but commonly skirmished in front of the main body, attacking the enemy here and there, and when hard pressed, retiring into the vacant spaces of the legion.

[7] On this side you stand: It was the custom for the patron, when acting as the counsel, to have his client standing by him while pleading. The wife complains that her father has been sent for by her to act as her own advocate, but that, instead of so doing, he is encouraging her supposed husband in his perverseness.

[8] A green colour: It was supposed that in madness, or extreme anger, the countenance assumed a greenish hue. Ben Jonson has probably imitated this passage in the Silent Woman, Act IV., sc. 4.: "Lord! how idly he talks, and how his eyes sparkle! he looks green about the temples! Do you see what blue spots he has?"

[9] Ho! Bromius: Evius and Bromius were two of the names by which the Bacchanals addressed Bacchus in their frenzy.

[10] Cygnus for his father: Plautus designedly makes Menaechmus Sosicles be guilty of the mistake of styling Tithonus the son of Cygnus, as helping to promote the belief of his madness. Tithonus was the son of Laomedon, and the brother of Priam. He was beloved by Aurora, and the poets feigned that he was her husband. Having received the gift of immortality, he forgot to have perpetual youthfulness united with the gift; and at length, in his extreme old age, he was changed into a grasshopper. There were several persons of the name of Cygnus, or Cycnus; one was the son of Apollo and Hyrie, another of Mars and Pelopea, or Pyrene, another of Neptune and Calyx, and a fourth of Ocitus and Arnophile.

[11] The rapid pace of your feet: "Cursu celeri facite inflexa sit pedum pernicitas." Literally, "in the swift course, make the swiftness of your feet to be bent inwards." The legs of good horses, when trotting fast, bend inwards before they throw them out.

[12] For Aesculapius: Apollo and Aesculapius were the two guardian Divinities of the medical art. The old man, perhaps, mentions their names instead of those of some persons of whose wonderful cures the Doctor has been bragging.

[13] Or a carpenter: He says that, talking of mending legs, the Doctor may, for aught he knows, be some carpenter, who has been patching up the legs of statues.

[14] Harassed by sprites: "Larvatus aut cerritus." The "larvati" were mad persons, supposed to be afflicted with ghosts or spectres; while the "cerriti" were persons who were thought to be visited with madness by the Goddess Ceres.

[15] Innumerable times as many: The Doctor is bragging of his extensive practice.

[16] My own Ulysses: He complains that the Parasite, who used to be his adviser, and as good as a Ulysses to him, his king, or patron, has been the cause of all his mishaps.

[17] Finish his life: "Vitâ evolvam suâ." Literally, "I will wind him off of his life." He probably alludes to the "Parcae," the "Fates" or "Destinies," who were fabled to be the daughters of Nox and Erebus, and of whom, one, named Clotho, held the distaff, and spun the thread of life; another, named Lachesis, wound it off; and the third, called Atropos, cut it off when of the requisite length.

[18] You are killing me: "Occidis fabulans." This remark seems rather to apply to the effect of his chattering, upon the old man himself, who is growing impatient, than upon the supposed madman; though, from the elliptical nature of the expression, the latter may possibly be the meaning.

[19] Of becoming hard: This was supposed to be one of the symptoms of madness.

[20] To be a locust: The eyes of locusts were considered to be of peculiar hardness. They are very large and prominent. It has been suggested that "locusta" here means a "lobster."

[21] That you stole: This expression has been already remarked upon in the Notes to the Trinummus.

[22] But, hanging up: "Pendentem." When they were flogged, the slaves were tied up with their hands extended over their heads. Probably, the Doctor is intended to be represented as being a slave; as many of the liberal pursuits were followed by slaves, and sometimes to the very great profit of their masters. The "furca" (for

want of a better word, called 'bilboes' in the translation) is referred to in another Note.

[23] That his back: For the purpose of keeping his back intact from the whip, and his feet from the fetters.

[24] Ground by myself: He alludes to the custom of sending refractory slaves to the "pistrinum," where the corn was ground by a handmill, which entailed extreme labour on those grinding. He says that he would rather that others should grind the corn for him, than that he should grind it for others.

[25] This thick wood: He compares the house of the Courtesan to a forest or thicket. These latter places, as being frequently the lurking-places of thieves and robbers, would be especially dangerous to travellers.

[26] If he does bring it: He contemplates robbing even the man who has just rescued him. The dishonesty of his brother, in carrying off the mantle and bracelet, and wishing to rob the servant-maid of the gold for her earrings, has been previously remarked.

[27] Better auspices: He alludes to the pretended manumission which he has already received from Menaechmus of Epidamnus, when he took him to be his master.

[28] Fifty hundred thousand: The sestertius, before the time of Augustus, was a silver coin of the value of twopence and one-half of a farthing; while after that period, its value was one penny three-farthings and a half. The large sum here mentioned, at the former value, amounts to 44,370£. 16s. 8d. He. says "vix," it will "hardly" amount, by way of a piece of boasting.

[29] Give us loud applause: This Comedy, which is considered to be one of the best, if not the very best, of all the plays of Plautus, is thought by some to have been derived from one of Menander's, as there are some fragments of a play by that Poet, called *Didumoi*, "the Twins." It is, however, very doubtful if such is the fact. It is rendered doubly famous from the fact that Shakespeare borrowed the plot of his Comedy of Errors from it, through the medium of the old translation of the Play, published in the year 1595, which is in some parts a strict translation, though in others only an

abridgment of the original work. It is thought to have been made by William Warner, who wrote a poem called "Albion's England," which he dedicated to Henry Cary, Lord Hunsdon, who was Lord Chamberlain to Queen Anne the wife of James the First.

THE END